Fully Revised and Updated Edition

Numerology

Know Your Lucky Numbers for Every Sphere of Life

Numerology

Know Your Lucky Numbers for Every Sphere of Life

By

V. Rajsushila

PUSTAK MAHAL®
Delhi • Bangalore • Mumbai • Patna • Hyderabad • London

Publishers
Pustak Mahal®, Delhi
J-3/16 , Daryaganj, New Delhi-110002
☎ 23276539, 23272783, 23272784 • *Fax:* 011-23260518
E-mail: info@pustakmahal.com • *Website:* www.pustakmahal.com

London Office
5, Roddell Court, Bath Road, Slough SL3 OQJ, England
E-mail: pustakmahaluk@pustakmahal.com

Sales Centre
10-B, Netaji Subhash Marg, Daryaganj, New Delhi-110002
☎ 23268292, 23268293, 23279900 • *Fax:* 011-23280567
E-mail: rapidexdelhi@indiatimes.com

Branch Offices
Bangalore: ☎ 22234025
E-mail: pmblr@sancharnet.in • pustak@sancharnet.in
Mumbai: ☎ 22010941
E-mail: rapidex@bom5.vsnl.net.in
Patna: ☎ 3294193 • *Telefax:* 0612-2302719
E-mail: rapidexptn@rediffmail.com
Hyderabad: *Telefax:* 040-24737290
E-mail: pustakmahalhyd@yahoo.co.in

ISBN 978-81-223-0006-2

Edition : 2007

Printed at : Param Offsetters, Okhla, New Delhi-110020

Contents

Preface

Numerology is the science of numbers which reveals their immense potentialities. Every human being has problems. The major problem is pain and sorrow and attainment of elusive pleasure and happiness. The only solution for this problem is approaching it in a numerological way and fixing a name on that basis. The science of numerology has the power to influence our lives, whether we believe in it or not, just as fire has the power to burn things whether we realise its power or not. Numbers have the power to rule us whether we believe in it or not.

The reason for disbelief in this science is lack of appreciation of the applicability of this science. In this book, I have given you proper knowledge of numerology, its origin and changing names appropriately. Alphabets and their sounds along with Nadi chakras have a close effect on human beings, characteristics of individuals born in different numbers, lucky and unlucky numbers, colours and their effects on human beings, selection of appropriate gem for every number and the rituals about wearing them, suitable mantras, tantras and remedial measures for negative numbers and so forth.

This book is most useful for business people, as I have explained the selection of business to each person according to his/her birth date and lucky and unlucky numbers in various types of businesses. I have also described the lucky days for wedding ceremonies, applying for a job or research in the educational field according to the birth date of each person.

I hope this book will guide readers and help them secure a bright future.

V. RAJSUSHILA
F-1, Arihant Ashoka Apt.,
Ashok Nagar,
Hyderabad-500 020, (A.P.) India
Ph: 27645532.

1

Origin of Numerology

Numerology is the science of numbers. It describes the forces behind numbers.

The first book on numerology was written by Cheiro. But even before Cheiro, there were some Brahmins of the Vedic times who were well versed in Numerical Science and were also scholars of Astronomy who knew about celestial bodies. These Brahmins came from generations of great Maharishis to whom Lord Dattathraya himself taught the numerical science based on the astronomical and planetary universe.

Cheiro, during his earlier life, when travelling in south India, came in contact with the Brahmins, who had all knowledge of this science.

These Brahmins were masters of the occult power of numbers in their application to time and in their relation to human life. But they hid the secrets from common people. However, they permitted Cheiro to learn certain theories on the occult nature of numbers, and the Sanskrit words related to them, planetary relationship of them, their influence over human life and so on. Cheiro, after grasping these secrets, returned to his native land. After several experimental applications of the numbers and their sound systems carefully, at last, he verified the English alphabets equivalent to such Sanskrit words taught by these Brahmins.

After coming to a conclusion, he released the secrets of the science of numbers, the sound force behind them, and the planetary influence over these numbers etc. to the world by writing a book on numerology.

The world came to know about numerology, and how it changes the luck of human beings.

Thus, the origin and place of birth of this science was ancient India only.

Even before Cheiro, John Heyden wrote a book "Holy Guide" regarding planets etc. Cheiro took the guidance of this book also and wrote the numerological book that was released first to the world. Once the book on the secrets of numbers was released, it spread the world over and, today, everybody is well informed about this science.

How Do Planets Influence Human Lives?

The universe exists in cosmic energy, which has powerful radiation. There are also other energies with their own radiation. The vibrational force emitted by each energy has an effect on the waves of other radiational energies. Although we cannot see these energies, we can feel them. For example, we have TV and radio waves all around us, but we do not see them. To know their existence, we have to switch them on. Only then can we pick up the waves transmitted. In the same manner, every human being emits rays of cosmic energies which we can know through the study of numerology only. The birth date determines the kind of rays which a person's planet emits. Each planet has been assigned a particular number. The moment a person is born, he is governed by a major and a minor planet, and begins to emit the vibrations of those two planets. First the major planet's vibration will start functioning. From the time he is given a name, the minor planet's vibration will also join in. The major planet is his birth planet, and the minor planet is his name and number planet. These two vibrational forces dominate his thinking, emotions, character, ambitions, likes, dislikes, health, career, luck etc. If these two planets' vibrational forces are in harmony, he will experience harmonious results. If, on the other hand, both of these vibrational forces are in opposition to each other, he will never live in harmony.

In this way, planets govern the fate and luck of human beings. With the help of numerology, one will be able to know which planet is harmonious and which is not, according to one's birth details. One will then be able to alter one's name suitably and come out of shoddy affairs. Numerology can guide people to shape their future and change their luck.

OOO

2

Effects of Numerology on Human Beings

The moment a man is born, he is governed by certain numbers. These numbers start influencing his life. He is identified only by a name and a number representing that name. Although he may not recognise them, he cannot escape the influence of that number.

As he grows older, year by year, numbers will be interwoven in his life. He will get success or failure, complete his education, and start his career according to the influence of the number on his life.

Numbers are very powerful and have divinity. Each number has a peculiar electromagnetic power by which the events in his life are profoundly influenced.

The chief number which influences or shapes a man's life is his birth number. The birth number has an influence on his mental capacity, profession, family background and all other incidents in his life.

According to the date of birth, there are 9 numbers—1 to 9—each of which is represented by a planet. The planets are assigned numbers. They are:

Sun	is assigned		No. '1'
Moon	is	"	No. '2'
Jupiter	is	"	No. '3'
Uranus	is	"	No. '4'
Mercury	is	"	No. '5'
Venus	is	"	No. '6'
Neptune	is	"	No. '7'
Saturn	is	"	No. '8'
Mars	is	"	No. '9'

Birth dates have their numbers. People are influenced and governed by planets which bear the numbers of their birth dates.

1. All those born on 1, 10, 19 or 28 of any month are dominated by number '1' planet Sun.

2. All those born on 2, 11, 20 or 29 of any month are dominated by No. '2' planet Moon.

3. All those born on 3, 12, 21 or 30 of any month are dominated by No. '3' planet Jupiter.

4. All those born on 4, 13, 22 or 31 of any month are dominated by No. '4' planet Uranus.

5. All those born on 5, 14, 23 of any month are dominated by No. '5' planet Mercury.

6. All those born on 6, 15 or 24 of any month are dominated by No. '6' planet Venus.

7. All those born on 7, 16, 25 of any month are dominated by No. '7' planet Neptune.

8. All those born on 8, 17 or 26 of any month are dominated by No. '8' planet Saturn.

9. All those born on 9, 18 or 27 of any month are dominated by No. '9' planet Mars.

In this manner, each number represents the influence of its dominating planet. A person's characteristics, personality and destiny are dominated by that planet. Persons born on a particular number (date) are influenced by the planet bearing that number. These planets have positive and negative effects on human beings. Positive effects work well if the name-number of a man is favourable to that planet or consistent with it. Negative effect prevails if the number is one of two or three bad numbers.

Depending on numbers, the effect on a person's destiny could be positive and beneficial or negative and destructive.

Positive Effects of No. 1: Self-confidence, originality, individuality, leadership, independence, enthusiasm, masculinity, creative ideas, power and position, quickness in decisions and carefulness.

Negative Effects of No. 1: Adamant, aggressive, egoistic, overconfident and unwilling to listen to others. Such a person cannot work under anyone because of bloated ego!

Positive Effects of No. 2: Diplomacy, love, motherly instincts, soothing conduct, cooperation, association, friendliness, healing, modesty, harmony, unity, appreciation of beauty and art, and favourable influence of occult and spiritual forces. Popular in social and romantic fields.

Negative Effects of No. 2: Oversensitive, easily hurt, delicate ego, shy, timid and dependent on encouragement for progress in work without which they can become negative.

Positive Effects of No. 3: Creative talents, imagination, good luck, cheerfulness, happiness, cleverness, confidence, ambition attracting success and money. Inspiration, creativity on the mental side, and in spiritual and philosophical endeavours of life, deep love and popularity, loyalty, sacrificing for the sake of love and eating and dressing well.

Negative Effects of No. 3: Bad moods, loss and disappointment, loose talks, unforgiving nature and always being critical of others.

Positive Effects of No. 4: Systematic, determined, efficient, calm, slow and steady, scientific, responsible, honest, faithful, carrying out tasks seriously, work-minded, active, selfless, principles-oriented, helpful and devoted to the family.

Negative Effects of No. 4: Lack of imagination, stubbornness, unwillingness to cooperate with others, argumentative nature, overseriousness, all work and no leisure.

Positive Effects of No. 5: Cleverness, dynamism, action-orientedness, love of change and freedom, amusement, entertainment, quick-wittedness, administrative capacity, indefatigable energy, business-mindedness, occult powers and religiousness.

Negative Effects of No. 5: Lack of concentration, restlessness, nervousness, discontentment, lustfulness, procrastination, infidelity, love of pleasure, wine, woman and distrust of others.

Positive Effects of No. 6: Sympathy, love, humanitarian service, loyalty, altruism, steadfastness, harmony, love of home, generosity, working for the well-being of others, co-operation, sense of responsibility, devotion to God, strong physique, intelligence, creativity, business sense, love of nature, honesty in money matters and spirituality.

Negative Effects of No. 6: Too much of duty consciousness and sacrifice, troubles to others, family ties, self-sacrifice, problems arising from straightforwardness, craving for recognition and being wedded to causes and consequent celibacy.

Positive Effects of No. 7: Analytical mind, interest in research, investigation, discovery and observation, intelligence, spiritual knowledge, excellent mental prowess, wisdom and knowledge, skilled work, specialisation, passionate interest, being charming, sincere and reserved.

Negative Effects of No. 7: Too much reservedness, lack of trust in others, aloofness, confusion, depression, pride, bad temper, irritability, argumentativeness and meanness.

Positive Effects of No. 8: Executive ability, authority, direction, supervision, efficiency, organisation, judgement, materialism, management, administrative competence, histrionic talent, success in a large organisation in industry, politics, engineering, or civil construction, flair for property dealings, printing and publishing, travel and tourism, sports, museums etc., intelligence, serviceableness, success in public speaking and scientific knowledge.

Negative Effects of No. 8: Over work and little time for personal matters, over ambitiousness, too much materialism, strain and tension, lack of humanitarianism towards others, impatience with others and tragedy of fate.

Positive Effects of No. 9: Selflessness, forgiveness, magnanimity, humanitarianism, tolerance, generosity, broadmindedness, charitable nature, philanthropic spirit, religiousness, dramatic talents, unorthodoxy, spirituality, propensity for divine life, skill, trustworthiness, loyalty, romanticism, working for others and good health.

Negative Effects of No. 9: Moody, hasty, unfaithful in love affairs and careless in money matters, selfish, intolerant, deceptive, inclined to high living and given to eating, drinking and merry-making.

Radiation of Numbers and Effects on Humans

1. The date of birth.
2. The name given to a person at the time of birth which is represented by a number. These are the two most important numbers that rule the life and destiny of an individual. These two numbers represent the two planets.

The date of birth of a person is his ruling number. It is considered his or her lucky number. Suppose the date of birth is 15-6-1948, we have to reduce this date to a single digit, 1+5 = 6. This number 6 is the ruling number of the person. All the dates of the month where the final digit comes to 6, such as 15 and 24, are lucky dates and the person should take all his important steps on these dates. Supposing he wants to ask for a favour from his seniors or he wants to advance in his career, or he submits an application for higher education, or performs something important or auspicious in his life—he should then select one of these dates for the purpose. If he wants to write an important letter, he should put this date on the letter.

Similarly, all the years in life where the final total after reducing it to a single digit is 6, are important years for that person and important or auspicious events usually take place during these years.

All these years of his life, he may complete his education, or he may his first job, or a promotion, or he may be married, or he may construct a new house, or he may have a child, or may get property and so on. Similarly, the critical number also plays an important role in a person's life. The total of all the numbers in a birth date is to be taken as the critical number. This is also called the destiny number. Suppose the birth date is 15-3-1948. We have to add all the digits in his birth date: 1+5+3+1+9+4+8 = 31.

Add 3+1 = 4. This 4 is called the critical number. This critical number repeats in the life of the person whether he likes it or not. The events may be either good or bad, and the person has no control over this number and the events. Suppose it is failure in business, or the winning of a prize. The date on which either of these events takes place will be governed by the number 4 in that case. The total of all the numbers of that date will be 4 or the number of the month when the incident took place will be 4.

Thus, the birth number and the critical number play an important role in a person's life.

3

The Alphabets & Numbers—Their Sound Value

The numbers and alphabets which influence human beings have planetary implications. Before explaining the same, I will explain how these numbers and alphabets influence human beings and how they influence the Nadi Chakras of the human body.

If a person pronounces the word "Cat", or if he reads it in a book, at once the picture of a Cat will come to mind. The meaning of the word 'Cat' is that picture. It means the word has the power to create the picture of a Cat in our minds. The word 'Cat' is formed by three alphabets "C, A and T" by pronouncing or writing these three alphabets one after another in the proper order, so that the letters denote 'Cat'.

If we alter this order and pronounce this word as "ACT", then the picture of a Cat will not be created in our minds. Hence the strength of the word 'Cat' is hidden within these three letters written in that order.

The first alphabet, the consequent second alphabet, and the third alphabet are formed on the basement of numbers 1, 2 and 3. Alphabets can create a word only if they are formed in the numerical order. Thus, the words are formed on the basis of a combination of numbers and alphabets.

The meaning of each such word is called 'Thought'. Numbers and alphabets are creating words as well as thoughts in our minds.

The deeds and activities of human beings are based on these thoughts. These deeds and activities are the reasons for good and bad. That is why our ancestors determined that the numbers and alphabets which create thoughts in our minds are the producers of good and bad for us.

The written form is called the 'alphabet'. The thought is called the 'number'. By means of this reference, you can understand the relation between the numbers and the alphabets. Alphabets have power.

By seeing a Cat, a man recognises that it is a Cat. Then he may not see the Cat for many years. After many years, if you talk to him about a Cat, at once the picture of a Cat which he saw a long time ago comes into his mind. All these years, this picture was hidden in the depths of his mind. After hearing the word 'Cat', the forgotten picture of the Cat at once appears in his mind. This is called memory power. The picture was hidden in the bottom of the mind all these years. This 'hiding' is termed forgetting.

In this manner:

A man recognised the Cat earlier, then forgot it, and once again remembered it. The power of remembering lies in the word 'Cat'. Ancient philosophers indicated this power as memory power. This is the power of alphabets.

Do alphabets lie only in the book and in spoken words? No. They lie in the bottom of our minds where our thoughts are hidden. It is this memory power of alphabets which enables us to remember forgotten things.

In the ancient Yoga Shastra, this 'thought' was described as 'Vaaq'. There are four kinds of Vaaq.

They are:

Para, Pashyanti, Madhyama, Vaikari.

When a thought turns into the form of a word, it is called Vaikari Vaaq.

There are two kinds of Vaikari Vaaq.

1. Sthoola Vaikari.
2. Sukshma Vaikari.

When thoughts turn into words through the mouth, they are called Sthoola Vaikari. The thought that lies only within the mind is called Sukshma Vaikari.

A man is walking through a forest. On the way, he sees a tiger. At once, what would he do?

Definitions of Vaaq

There is a yellowish liquid matter (yolk) inside an egg. This is the matter that later turns into a chick. Similarly, instinct becomes a thought in the later stage. Ancient saints called this instinct Madhyama Vaaq.

This Madhyama Vaaq forms into Sthoola Vaikari and Sukshma Vaikari in the next stage.

What is the difference between the yolk and the chick? It is the same difference between Madhyama Vaaq and Vaikari Vaaq. A chick knows about its body. But it does not know about the yolk, which is the origin of its body. In the same manner, we can well recognise our thoughts when it is in the form of Vaikari Vaaq. But we cannot recognise Madhyama Vaaq which is the origin of this Vaikari Vaaq thought.

Birds and animals act directly through Madhyama Vaaq (that means 'Instinct') without any obstacles of Vaikari Vaaq. But they also cannot recognise Madhyama Vaaq. Only great saints, who possess Yogasiddhi, are able to recognise this Madhyama Vaaq.

Vaikari Vaaq lies in our throat. Madhyama Vaaq lies inside the heart. Under Madhyama Vaaq lies Pashyanti Vaaq in the stomach. Para Vaaq lies beneath it. These are related to the Nadi Chakras in our body.

There are seven Nadi Chakras in our body. Of the seven, four are in the trunk of the body, two in the head and one in the neck.

Chakra is the power centre associated with the subtle body of man. Each chakra is ruled by an incarnation of Goddess Parashakti.

1. **Sahasrara Chakra:** It is the crown chakra above the head.

2. **Ajna Chakra:** This part is ruled by Yakini Devi. It lies between the eyebrows. It is ruled by Hakini Devi.

3. **Vishuddhi Chakra:** Situated in the neck at the vocal chords. This is the chakra that controls Vaikari Vaaq. It is controlled by Dakini Devi.

4. **Anaahata Chakra:** It lies inside the heart. It controls Madhyama Vaaq. It is ruled by Rakini Devi.

5. **Manipura Chakra (Nabhi Chakra):** It lies in the stomach. This is ruled by Lakini Devi.

6. **Svadishthana Chakra:** It lies in the lower stomach. It controls Pashyanti Vaaq. It is ruled by Kakini Devi.

7. **Mooladhara Chakra:** It lies in the kidney. It controls Para Vaaq. It is ruled by Sakini Devi.

Of these seven chakras, the Sahasrara and Ajna Chakras are the highest chakras, related to Yogasiddhi.

The other five chakras are controlled by Panchabhootaas in our body.

Vishuddhi Chakra is controlled by Aakash, Anaahata Chakra by Vaayu, Manipura Chakra by Agni, Svadishthana Chakra by Water and Mooladhara by Earth.

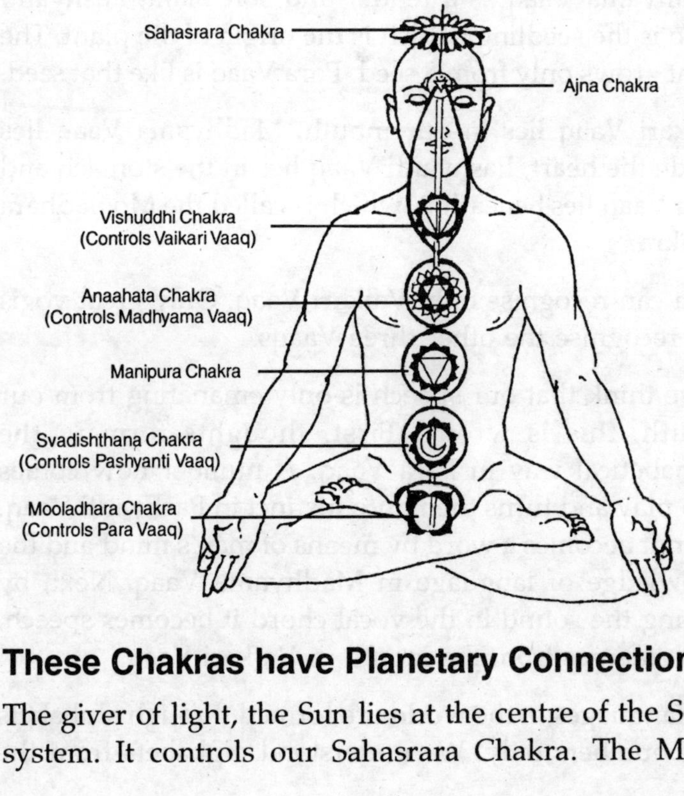

These Chakras have Planetary Connections

The giver of light, the Sun lies at the centre of the Solar system. It controls our Sahasrara Chakra. The Moon reflects the light of the Sun situated in between our eyebrows where we reflect. It controls the Vishuddhi Chakra.

Mercury controls our speech. Speech is the communicating link. It is situated in the neck at the vocal chords, the connecting centre of the body. Similarly, Anaahata, Manipura, Svadishthana and Mooladhara Chakra are also ruled by other planets.

Thus the chakras are responsible for producing sound alphabets and numbers in our body which are ruled by planets.

Madhyama Vaaq is very tender. Pashyanti Vaaq is even more tender than Madhyama Vaaq. If we describe Madhyama Vaaq as a tender and soft plant, Pashyanti Vaaq is the seedling, which is the origin of the plant. The plant grows only from a seed. Para Vaaq is like that seed.

Vaikari Vaaq lies in our mouth, Madhyama Vaaq lies inside the heart, Pashyanti Vaaq lies in the stomach and Para Vaaq lies beneath it, which is called the Mooladhara Chakra.

Man can recognise only Vaikari Vaaq. Only great yogis can recognise the other three Vaaqs.

If we think that our speech is only emanating from our mouth, this is wrong. First, thoughts form in the alphabetical way in Para Vaaq. A number now comes into play and turns them into instinct in Pashyanti Vaaq. Then it becomes a word by means of man's mind and the knowledge of language in Madhyama Vaaq. Next, by joining the sound in the vocal chord it becomes speech, and emerges from the mouth in Vaikari Vaaq.

All languages in the world are formed through alphabets and numbers only. We understand alphabets from the words released through our mouth. But numbers are hidden behind them. These are mixed invisibly in Para Vaaq. That is why the Shastras reveal that alphabets are hidden inside our heart. Goddess Parashakti lies in the Mooladhara of human beings in the form of Para Vaaq and she creates thoughts in man. She controls his speech, which derives from alphabets.

These three Vaaqs in our body are controlled by Parashakti, the goddess of creation, protection and destruction. Parashakti controls Vaaqs by means of three powers—the 'Ichcha Shakti', 'Jnana Shakti' and 'Kriyashakti'—through the nine planets. Hence it is understood that each alphabet is a Beejakshara and a powerful mantra.

Alphabets & the Planets

What is the relation between these alphabets and numbers with the planets? The Panchabhootaas which are in the outside world also lie inside our body. This is called the "Sukshmaloka". The outside Sukshmaloka controls the inside Sukshmaloka. The inner Sukshmaloka creates the thoughts and activities of man. Man is the leader of this inner Sukshmaloka, whereas planets are leaders of the outside loka. That is why planets affect all our activities and also our destiny. Planets bearing the same numbers rule over men who have similar numbers either in their dates of birth or in the alphabets of their names. Planets have the power to create and control thoughts, activities, and destinies through these numbers and alphabets of names. In the inner Sukshmaloka alphabets and sounds play an important part. That is why they are given numbers such as 1, 2, 3 and so on. But in the outside Sukshmaloka, planets play vital roles. That is why planets were given numbers by our ancestors.

Sun's number is	1
Moon's number is	2
Mars' number is	9
Mercury's number is	5
Jupiter's number is	3
Venus' number is	6
Saturn's number is	8
Rahu's number is	4
Ketu's number is	7

There are seven days in a week. Each day was given a planet's name. For Sunday the name of Sun, for Monday the name of Moon, for Tuesday the name of Mars, for Wednesday the name of Budha, for Thursday the name of Brihaspati, for Friday the name of Venus, for Saturday the name of Saturn. In this way, each day was given a particular planet's name.

What is the relation between these planets and the days of the week? We are living on planet Earth. The Sun lies at the centre of the universe. The other planets rotate around the Sun. While rotating around the Sun, each planet comes in close contact with the Earth on a particular day of the week. The day when a planet comes close to the Earth is named after that planet. When the Sun comes close on a particular day, the day is Sunday. When the Moon comes close on a particular day, the day is Monday and so on.

The ancient saints have given numbers to planets on the basis of the rotation of those planets, the distance between the Earth and the planets, and the way of their contact with the Earth.

The planet which rules the date of birth of a human being is responsible for the nature, character, activities, education, job, money and all his fortunes. It is the planet which bestows fortune on him. If his name is in that planet's number or its favourable or friendly number, the planet showers ample fortune on him. If it is an opposite planet's name, or an inimical planet's name, then he will have to grapple with misfortune. Hence the name of a person should be in a favourable alphabetic number. Numerology will thus help him amass riches, if the person's naming is done thoughtfully or imaginatively.

OOO

4

Characters of People Born on Various Numbers

No. 1

All those born on the 1st, 10th, 19th and 28th of any month are governed by the number 1 and this is their ruling number.

Characteristics

They have ego and self-respect and don't fear anything. There is transparency and honesty in them. They will be the centres of attraction in any society. They are brave and not afraid to put forth their views. They have high ideals in life with character. They are articulate and outspoken. They become impatient when faced with competition or delay. They go straight to the point with courage and confidence. They have originality, drive and dynamism. They are attracted to mental rather than physical work. Hence they are associated with learning, teaching and training of others. They have the opportunity to hold executive and administrative positions. They have flair for writing, literary pursuits and journalism and have contact with newspapers and the like.

Financial Matters

Their financial stability will be delayed. They will normally experience financial stability from their 37th year. They will achieve financial success through their own intelligence.

In the course of their career, they are likely to make many bitter enemies.

Health

They usually have weak eyesight. Their complaints are mainly psychological, and they usually suffer from depression, insomnia and nervousness. Their over-anxiety often creates indigestion and irregular and erratic blood circulation.

Remedy

Honey and milk are good as regular items of food. Barley water, orange, lemon, dates and ginger are good for them.

Married Life

No. 1 Husband: He is generous and desires his wife to shine in society. He wants his family members to act according to his will and will never tolerate anyone flouting his word. He is kind and noble-hearted. He loves his home and spends much of his time at home.

He is an emotional person and a dreamer! He likes to have a wife with an attractive personality, charming manners and intelligence.

No. 1 Wife: She is a good companion to her husband. She is intelligent. Her home is a social centre. She is friendly in manners, aristocratic by her dignity and attracts people at her home and commands great respect. Her interests are wide. She takes interest in the business of her husband.

She pays attention to the welfare of her husband and children.

No. 2

All those born on the 2nd, 11th, 20th and 29th of any month are governed by the number 2 and this is their ruling number.

Characteristics

They are pleasant and very imaginative. They worry a lot about imaginary problems. They are dreamy natured and build castles in the air!

False notions of ghosts etc. and fear of them are characteristics of such persons. They often go off mood, and even a trivial matter upsets them and they fight. They are selfless and always mindful of the well-being of others. They love neatness. They love the sea, flowers, sky, and scenery and natural beauty. They love change. Therefore they like long travel, which satisfies them.

Financial Matters

They are the lazy type—not capable of doing hard work. They are unstable in mind, which disturbs their routine work. They normally attain success after the 38th year, avoid speculation and shy away from risks.

They may acquire wealth and property by their own efforts or through marriage.

Health

They normally suffer from improper blood circulation. This gives rise to anaemia and weakness. They always suffer from uneasiness, worry and sleeplessness. They are susceptible to diabetes, asthma or respiratory problems.

Disorder of the kidneys, sore throat, intestinal or stomach disorders may also occur.

Remedy

Eschewing too much coffee or tea or other drinks.

Take cucumber, cabbage and other water-rich vegetables.

Married Life

No. 2 Husband: There are two types of number 2 husbands.

1st Type: Domineering and critical. Nothing satisfies him. He wants everything to be given to him without asking for it.

2nd Type: Lazy and dull. He marries for the sake of money, so that he gets comforts. He has love and attraction for the home, and likes the company of his children.

He likes his wife to have an attractive personality, good manners and intelligence.

No. 2 Wife: She is sympathetic and affectionate. She is satisfied with anything her husband provides her with. However she is moody, changeable and sensitive. She is friendly in manners. She has a great feeling of comfort and decorates her home in luxurious way. However, she is lazy and spends her time in an idle way. She is patient and can adjust to circumstances.

No. 3

All those born on the 3rd, 12th, 21st or 30th of any month are governed by the number 3, and this is their ruling number.

Characteristics

There will be sympathy and warmth in their talk. They are ready to sacrifice for the good of others. Their talks are authoritative.

They have high self-esteem and are proud. When they receive any help from others, they feel there is some weakness in them. They dress well and like to take a leading part in social organisations. They have a wide circle of friends. They have morals and all the good things attract them. They have strong desire for peace and harmony. They are confident about their own ability and make their own decisions.

Financial Matters

In financial matters, they are very lucky. They will get all comforts in life by their enthusiasm. They are out of poverty early. They should not lend money without security, otherwise they may risk losing it. They are very fortunate in business, finance and industry.

Health

They are liable to suffer chest disorders, throat infections, sudden fever, sore throat and rheumatic troubles as well.

They also often have pain in the feet. Undue anxiety often creates indigestion. Skin eruptions are also common with these people.

Remedy

Take Anar regularly. You can take Madipala Rasayanam which is best suited. Apple, Saffron, Beetroot, Wheat and Podina are good for their health.

Married Life

No. 3 Husband: He likes his wife to be attractive with pleasing manners and intelligence. He is loving by nature. He generally marries a girl above his economic status. He is attracted to beauty, and usually gets a good-looking wife.

No. 3 Wife: She is the best companion to her husband. She is efficient in house keeping, and sympathetic and caring towards her children.

She is better adapted to family life. She likes a luxurious life and desires her home to be a heaven. She is devoted, kind, sympathetic, but easy-going.

No. 4

All those born on the 4th, 13th, 22nd or 31st of any month are governed by the number 4 and ruled by this number.

Characteristics

They are always moody. When their mood is upset, it takes them a long time to recover from depression and regain cheerfulness.

They work long hours but gain little appreciation. Women born on this date will work hard at home and take the responsibilities of the whole family. They are trustworthy and earn a good reputation in society.

Financial Matters

Their financial prosperity usually starts from the age of 40. In financial matters, they may experience many sudden and unexpected changes.

It is better for them to work alone. They will be successful while working alone. If they have partners, they will be suspicious of the persons associated with them. These people should always be careful in their behaviour with employees, servants and inferiors. They may ill-treat them often.

Health

Their respiratory system will usually be weak and they may suffer from breathlessness. Knees and feet are affected. Sudden stomach pain may afflict them often. Sometimes, they suffer from urinary infections. Their complaints are difficult to diagnose. Anaemia and mental sickness are also likely.

Remedy

They should stop worrying. That is the best remedy. They should not take non-vegetarian food because their digestive organs are always weak. They should always take soup of any digestive mixture.

Married Life

No. 4 Husband: They are cunning, intelligent and expect wives to share their views. They are domineering. They want the home to be run as per their ideas. They are kind and loving. But they are always critical of everything, and this could create tension in the family.

No. 4 Wife: They are smart and attractive. They have strong will power. They dress well. They are dictatorial. They are always restless and moody. They love their homes, but are not attached to it very much.

No. 5

All those born on the 5th, 14th, or 23rd of any month are governed by the number 5 and this is their ruling number.

Characteristics

They are active and always like changes in the surroundings, ideas, dress, arrangement of furniture at home, friendship etc.

They assess everything in terms of money only. Their grasping power is fast. They love travel. They have fluency in writing or speaking. They never lose heart when they confront failure. They easily overcome the same and choose another way. They earn well, and spend on religious matters. They have faith in God. Their inner advice is the best guide to them.

Financial Matters

They are lucky in money matters. They are capable of developing their own business and carry out their plans systematically and get good returns. They are successful in any business. They are clever, but bad acquaintances may drag them into trouble before they realise their undesirable influence.

They are good at investments and speculations.

Health

They always suffer from nervousness. With the increase of tension, this nervousness will increase.

Remedy

They should take adequate rest and avoid drinks, night shows etc. Consuming carrots, nuts and peas are good for them. They should take B-complex regularly.

Married Life

No. 5 Husband: He selects a wife of his own choice. He expects her to be neat and tidy. He likes to see her well dressed. He loves his children and is fond of home and eager to return to his home. He is liberal in spending on clothes and other wants of family members. He furnishes his house with elegant taste.

No. 5 Wife: She is a fine companion. She is intelligent and friendly. Her interests are wide. She pays full attention to the welfare of her husband and children. She engages in many activities and has interests at home as well as outside which she manages well.

No. 6

All those born on the 6th, 15th, or 24th of any month are governed by the number 6 and it is their ruling number.

Characteristics

They are passionate. They are fond of new clothes and like to wear costly dresses. They adorn their homes with divine pictures and like attraction in everything. They are clean. They want harmony and peace. They are trustworthy. They have more feminine qualities, sympathy and love. They have sharp memory. They get success in speculation. Accumulation of money is not their aim and they acquire whatever interests them.

Financial Matters

Their interest is directed towards attaining pleasures and gratifying their desires. Money comes to them in unexpected ways. They are fortunate in financial matters. They get help and assistance from their relatives and friends in times of difficulties. They may make profits through gifts etc. They may gain financially through marriage. They make good investments in houses, land and property.

Health

Fever and influenza affect them. Nervousness and rheumatism are also common to these people.

Remedy

They should take honey daily. Anar, podina, beans, almond and watermelon are good for them. Gulkand is very good for their health.

Married Life

No. 6 Husband: He expects his partner to be neat and have charm and grace. He loves his children and home. He is very kind, generous and devoted. Art is everything to him. He desires to have a wife he can be proud of.

No. 6 Wife: She is a devoted mother and loving wife. She loves domestic life and is a perfect homemaker. She is a fine companion, intelligent and kind-hearted. She makes others jealous by her behaviour. She endures extreme hardships for the sake of her husband.

No. 7

All those born on the 7th, 16th, or 25th of any month are governed by the number 7, their ruling number.

Characteristics

They are punctual. They like the right order in everything. They are not articulate. They lead others well. They are stubborn and disregard the opinion of others. They dislike mingling with common people. They like freedom and even break the traditional bondage. Their behaviour is a mystery to others. They are often absent-minded.

Financial Matters

They will find a job of their own choice. They may be wealthy persons with all comforts, but they should be cautious while lending money. They may not get it back easily. Monetary stability may be at stake. But ultimately they will get success and command all comforts in life.

Health

They are prone to sickness on account of nervousness. Stomach disorders and rheumatism are also common. They get tired easily as a result of continuous work. They always suffer from weakness of the intestines. They should be very careful. They always suffer from mental depression, skin ailments and constipation.

Remedy

They should avoid drugs and drinks. Fruit juice, water-rich vegetables and buttermilk are good. They should take only light food at night.

Married Life

No. 7 Husband: He is emotional but understands the feelings of his wife. He is liberal, and fond of picnics, travel and cinema. Usually he is suspicious of his wife. He is critical about everything and that creates tension for family members. Nothing satisfies him. He is a spendthrift and likes to live lavishly. He has all comforts in life. He is domineering.

No. 7 Wife: She is always moody. Her behaviour is unpredictable. She gets disturbed over even trivial matters and becomes restless. She expects her husband to look after her all the time. She always likes to be alone, and does not mix with others.

No. 8

All those born on the 8th, 17th, or 26th of any month are governed by the number 8, their ruling number.

Characteristics

Their brain is active and sharp. They weigh their speech carefully. They are patient and untiring. They work for long on a problem. They show an extreme sense of discipline and dutifulness. They are the solitary type. They love music but mostly melancholic. They are cautious about their future and take decisions thoughtfully. They are creative, productive and domineering. They usually feel lonely at heart. They are likely to be misunderstood.

Financial Matters

There is delay in achieving financial stability, which they achieve rather late in life. They should work hard to get rich. They should be cautious about financial matters. They trust very few. Despite these precautions, they incur losses and are robbed by their servants. They can make money by investment in old, established concerns, the fruit trade and also in business connected with land, houses, mines and minerals.

Health

They should avoid drugs of all kinds. Otherwise, they may get liver trouble. They should be careful about their diet and keep their intestines in good condition, or they will be liable to acute poisoning, constipation, boils, skin eruptions and the like.

Nervousness, troubles of leg, teeth and the ear are the norm. They take long to cure.

Remedy

They ought to avoid non-vegetarian food completely. They should take light food at night. They may take banana, palakura carrot, orange juice etc. for their health.

Married Life

No. 8 Husband: Usually, he does not have any desire to get married, and is not much attracted to girls. He prefers to be alone. Even if he marries, it is at a very late age. He often makes his married life miserable. He is very orthodox and does not allow his wife to have modern ideas or wear modern dresses. This creates disappointment in his wife and a dislike for her husband. If he wants a happy married life, he should select a wife who would like to devote herself to philosophy.

No. 8 Wife: She has a masculine personality. She is systematic, enjoys family life and likes to make sacrifices for her children and husband. She lacks feminine warmth, delicacy and sentiment.

No. 9

All those who are born on the 9th, 18th or 27th of any month are governed by the number 9, their ruling number.

Characteristics

They are brave. They face any situation in life. They have endurance and usually adapt to any circumstances.

They are more likely to be strict than kind. A rule is a rule, there is no drifting away from it. They are always aggressive and will not stop until they achieve their goal. They will not accept defeat. They do not have weak sentiments. They have sympathy for the poor. They love children and animals. They are fond of the family. They usually lead a good married life despite their bad temper.

Financial Matters

They are lucky in money matters. They earn more than an average person. They are liberal in spending. They enjoy all the comforts that money can buy.

Health

They suffer from heart troubles, bronchitis and allergies. Boils due to excess of heat or skin eruptions are likely.

Remedy

They should take fruit, milk and buttermilk regularly. They should take a head bath regularly.

Married Life

No. 9 Husband: He is fond of a good-looking wife, family and children and would like to have a good house. He is always suspicious of his wife.

No. 9 Wife: She is a witty and clever conversationalist. She is an ambitious person and will assist her husband in his business.

OOO

5

The Lucky and Unlucky Numbers of Planets

The nine planets are represented by nine numbers. The planets as well as the numbers have harmonious vibrations with certain other planets and numbers. They are the lucky numbers of those planets.

Similarly, certain other planets, known as inimical planets, have bad vibrations with those planets. They are the unlucky numbers of those planets.

Numbers	Planet	Lucky Numbers	Unlucky Numbers
1.	Sun	1, 2, 3, 5, 9	6, 8
2.	Moon	1, 2, 4, 6	3, 5, 7, 8, 9
3.	Jupiter	1, 3, 9	2, 4, 5, 6, 7, 8
4.	Rahu	1, 2, 4, 5, 6	3, 7, 8, 9
5.	Mercury	1, 4, 5, 7, 8, 6	2, 9
6.	Venus	2, 4, 5, 6, 7, 8, 9	1, 3
7.	Ketu	1, 2, 5, 6, 7, 8	3, 4, 9
8.	Saturn	5, 7, 8, 6	1, 2, 3, 4, 9
9.	Mars	1, 3, 6, 9	2, 4, 5, 7, 8

How to Find Them and Know Their Effects on Humans

Suppose a person is born on 1st, 10th, 19th, 28th. He can keep his name in the number of 1, 10, 19, 29 or 3, 12, 21, 30 or 5, 14, 23 and 9, 18, 27. This can produce luck for him. Similarly, if he keeps his name in 6, 15, 24 or 8, 17, 26 it will bi:ing him bad luck. In the same way, you can see the above list and know which numbers and planets are lucky for you and which are inimical or hostile.

6

Colours and the Effect of Planets on Them, and Colours for Various Occasions

In numerology, just like numbers and alphabets, gems also play an important role.

Each planet likes a particular colour. The Sun likes the colour orange, Moon likes white, Mars likes red, Mercury likes green, Venus blue, Rahu the colour of Gomeda and Ketu the colour of Vaidurya.

According to numerology, if a man is governed by the Sun, he should always think about the Sun's colour, i.e. orange. That means, whatever object he sees in front he should imagine and see it in orange colour.

If a person thinks in this manner, his difficulties and ill health will be over. His fear will vanish. He will regain peace of mind. Whatever work he embarks upon, he will be successful. He will achieve happiness in life.

But it is very difficult for a man to always think about a specific colour. It requires great practice to see and think of a particular colour and then imagine it as another colour. This kind of practice is so hard. So the ancient saints discovered an easy way out. The colour of the gem we want to think of is fixed in a ring which we can wear on our finger. If we often see that ring on our finger, the cosmic rays of the planet which attract that colour produce vibrational powers. These vibrations will bring good luck to us. It is in this way that the use of lucky gems started. Thus, colours are very important, and wearing of a gem is also based on this principle.

The Importance of Using Colours and Gems

Our body is composed of seven primary colours of the solar spectrum, viz. violet, indigo, blue, green, yellow, orange and red. These are called the primary colours. When there is deficiency or absence of any of these primary colours in our body, we are attacked with the disease caused by its deficiency. Suppose red rays are absent, diseases like fever, anaemia, physical debility, loss of vitality and weakness afflict our body. These diseases can be cured by injecting red rays into our body by wearing gems of red planets. The red planets are Sun and Mars. Their gems are ruby and red coral. When we wear these gems, they come into contact with our body, thereby the deficiency is corrected and we become free from these diseases.

Similarly, by wearing a ruling planet's gem or a favourable planet's gem, one can get rid of bad luck and experience good luck in life. In this way, colours and the relevant gems can change our bad fate also. Gems are credited with latent powers as well. They are worn to guard against the evil influences of planets. A natural efficacy exists in them for the cure of certain diseases as well as for neutralising the evil effects of planets on human beings. If planetary vibrations are negative, these negative currents are required to be neutralised with positive ones and gemstones serve the purpose.

Colours for Various Occasions

The Sun's favourite colour is red and orange. So persons born on 1, 10, 19, or 28 are governed by the Sun and should use orange or red colour for luck. The gem for them is Ruby.

Persons born on 2, 11, 20, or 29 are governed by the Moon. They should use white colour for luck. The gem for them is pearl or moonstone, which can infuse white rays into the body.

Persons born on 3, 12, 21, or 30 are governed by the planet Jupiter. They should use yellow colour for luck. The gem they need is yellow Pushyarag.

Persons born on 4, 13, 22, or 31 are governed by the planet Uranus. They ought to use the colour of Gomeda for luck. Their gem is Gomeda. Persons born on 5, 14, or 23 are governed by the planet Mercury, and they should use green colour for luck. They need to wear emerald.

Persons born on 6, 15, or 24 are governed by the planet Venus and they should use the colour blue for luck. Their gem is the blue diamond.

Persons born on 7, 16, or 25 are governed by the planet Neptune and they should use the colour of the cat's eye for luck. The gem best suited for them is cat's eye.

Persons born on 8, 17, or 26 are governed by the planet Saturn and they should use the colour dark blue for luck. They need blue sapphire.

Persons born on 9, 18, or 27 are governed by the planet Mars, and they should use the colour red for luck. Their gem is the red coral.

It is clear that gemstones cure diseases and bring happiness and prosperity.They are used not only for protection from the evil influences of planets but also to neutralise the evil effects of hostile planets on human beings.

OOO

7

Qualities of Single Numbers from 1 to 9

In a person's horoscope each number casts a negative or positive influence. If a number is in a good position, it is called a positive position. It means the planet which indicates that particular number is in a positive position capable of producing good effects. Similarly, when a number is in a negative position, it means the planet it denotes is in a negative position and capable of affecting the person adversely. In a person's horoscope, the nine planets produce good and bad effects according to their positions in the horoscope and the numbers associated with the planets.

The Good and Bad Effects of No. 1

Good Effects: Elevation of status, promotion or improved authority, name and fame, acquisition of properties, vehicles and the like.

Bad Effects: It causes trouble at the workplace. Seniors give much trouble in the office. Sometimes, these people are misunderstood and suspended from service under trying circumstances or they themselves may quit the job. False cases may also be launched against them. Sometimes, separation from the family may take place too.

The Good and Bad Effects of No. 2

Good Effects: The person will inherit the parents' property. Children may be born. Marriage may be celebrated. Chances of promotion or transfer are also indicated. Change of place is also on the cards. He may go abroad or may have overseas contacts bringing him prosperity.

Bad Effects: This may adversely affect the mind. Fear, worry, anxiety, sleeplessness, etc. are also indicated. It may cause quarrels between husband and wife and make them separate. They may be compulsorily transferred from service. The person does not have shame or sympathy and may lack concentration in the chosen activity or business.

The Good and Bad Effects of No. 3

Good Effects: Marriage, childbirth, house property, improvement in business, name and fame, overseas trips for higher education and so forth.

Bad Effects: Obstacles to work on hand, failure in the attempts, monetary loss in business and the possibility of being cheated are some of the likely bad effects of the planet. He has to beware of cheats, including partners. Although he is talented, he may be too shy to reveal it due to lack of self-confidence. He may hurt the feelings of others by sheer inadvertence.

The Good and Bad Effects of No. 4

Good Effects: Position, success in business, abundance of money and unexpected successes are some of the benefits on the cards.

Bad Effects: There may be undue control or interference by others. Bonded labour may occasion court proceedings against him. He may lose money or wealth. Whatever work he undertakes, he may not complete it. The person may even go underground. Name and fame may be in peril. He may get embroiled in vexatious litigation. Loss of reputation and dishonour could lead to bouts of depression, culminating even in suicide.

The Good and Bad Effects of No. 5

Good Effects: It can make people cooperative with him. It may improve his business. He may achieve name and fame. Marriages may take place.

Bad Effects: The person may wander aimlessly, deceive others, shirk responsibility, commit theft, indulge in smuggling and gambling and ruin himself by excessive drinking. It may lead the person to do illegal business and thereby involve him in cases. Sometimes, it can even enmesh the person in affairs with women and thereby drag him into serious problems.

If it is a woman, she may dislike domestic chores. If it is a man, he may shirk his domestic responsibilities. Wine and woman may prove his weakness and undoing.

The Good and Bad Effects of No. 6

Good Effects: Marriages may take place. Other benefits may be childbirth, happy married life, construction of house, acquisition of property, and substantial savings. He may live very happily and do charities. He may become deeply religious, generous, sympathetic and cooperative towards everyone in the family.

Bad Effects: Wandering and drinking may ruin the person. It may make the person marry thoughtlessly in haste and come to serious trouble. A long battle for separation may ensue, culminating in eventual divorce.

He may take it into his head to deceive others but may jeopardise his own money and may have to work hard for others.

The Good and Bad Effects of No. 7

Good Effects: He may turn philosophical. He may become brilliant and impress others with his character. He may study very well indeed and come first in exams. He may achieve an eminent position, do research and may go abroad for higher studies, research or training.

Bad Effects: It may make him aggressive, he may deceive others and hurt their feelings. He may exert very hard and yet not come by riches.

Sometimes, he may not get any job on account of a misunderstanding or serious differences with family members. He may flee home. He may stay single for too long and even if married, he may not take interest in the family. He may never help anyone. He may not have a friend and may keep aloof from others.

The Good and Bad Effects of No. 8

Good Effects: He may have bright business prospects. Administrative competence may take him to the highest position. He may achieve success in education, particularly in technical education and this could boost his career. He may engage in spiritual pursuits and even become devout and philanthropic.

Bad Effects: He may get embroiled in fights. He may be easily provoked. He may become stubborn. He may get entangled in serious cases. He may incur serious loss of money in the business. He may incur debt and may be prone to diseases and troubles. He may become penniless. He may even be jailed!

The Good and Bad Effects of No. 9

Good Effects: Marriage, childbirth, name and fame, property, vehicles, good health, charity, becoming spiritual and sympathetic, the possibility of earning wealth are some of the benefits which may be expected.

Bad Effects: It may make the man a ringleader and a rowdy. He may get embroiled in criminal cases. His health may be in jeopardy. It can even separate husband and wife. Outbreak of fire and accident are other possibilities.

OOO

8

Numerology & Gems

Selection of Appropriate Gems for Various Numbers & Rituals for Wearing Them

Beneficial Effects of Gems

Gems and their beneficial uses have been mentioned in the Vedas and Puranas. In Brihat Samhita it is described at length. Ancient books on medicine like Bhava Prakash, Ayurveda Prakash and Rasa Ratna have also described the value and use of gems. It is believed that gems can cure some of the deadliest diseases.

How Gems Bring Good Luck

The Earth has greater gravitational force than the other planets. Due to this gravitational force, a huge amount of cosmic rays of the planets falls on the earth. These rays fall on human beings who live on earth. Such rays produce many effects on the physical and mental conditions of human beings. By virtue of these effects, many incidents occur in his life. Every incident involving a human being is a reflection of his thoughts only. As his thought is, so will be the incidents. Hence the nine planets by means of their cosmic rays influence human minds and thoughts, causing good and bad luck to them.

Generally, cosmic rays of all planets produce negative vibrations. These negative vibrations create bad effects on human beings. Though all the planets' vibrations affect human beings, the birth planet's rays always surround him invisibly. These can also be negative vibrations. Gems have the power of transforming these negative vibrations into positive ones. They may offset the evil vibrations and as a result only good vibrations may affect human bodies, thereby producing good luck. As the umbrella protects us from the severe heat of summer, and from rain in the rainy season, so the gem protects us from the rays of the planets, neutralises evil vibrations and directs only the good vibrations towards our body. In this way, it works as a shield and protects us. Wearing of a lucky gem not merely changes our bad luck into good, but also cures our ill health and brings about success in finance, business, job, education, and marriage, and confers peace of mind. You will be surprised to know how it is possible to gain a planet's strength through a tiny gemstone. Yes—it is possible. Just as we are directing the TV through a remote control and just as fixed cameras in the space rocket are directed through an electronic computer, so also we can attract the rays of a particular planet to a gem.

Appropriate Gems

Our body is composed of seven colours. They are called the 'Indradhanush' in the Shastras. These colours should be in equal amounts in our body. If any colour is deficient, our health will suffer. We should then inject rays of the deficient colour into our body by means of the gem, which picks up the concerned planet's colour rays and radiates them into our body. Planets are in different colours and each emits rays of its own colour to the Earth. Different gems capture and radiate them into our body.

The Sun and Mars throw red rays, and gems like ruby, golden topaz, red coral and garnet can capture these red rays and inject them into our body. Mercury throws green rays, and emerald, and other green stones can capture the green rays and radiate them into our body.

Saturn throws blue rays, and blue sapphire and other blue gems can capture blue rays from Saturn and inject them into our body. Similarly, Jupiter throws yellow rays. Yellow sapphire, yellow topaz and other yellow gems can capture and inject yellow rays into our body. When the gem injects the deficient colour into our body, these rays mix into our body, correct the deficiency of that colour and make it balanced. Then our health will be restored.

Similarly, if any colour is found in excess in our body, it will also be controlled and balanced by wearing the particular gem. In this way, gems control the colours in our body, and make them balanced, which is a *sine qua non* for good health.

If any colour is deficient in our body it is described in science as 'mineral deficiency'. These Navaratnas introduce mineral powers into our body and also make it balanced with the minerals in question.

Selection of Appropriate Gem

The selection of an appropriate gem can be done through numerology.

All those born on 1, 10, 19, or 28 of any month are ruled by the Sun. The gemstone which produces the strength of the Sun is ruby.

They should wear ruby. It is usually in red colour. Wearing of ruby confers wealth and attraction too on the wearer.

All those born on 2, 11, 20, or 29 of any month are ruled by the moon. The gemstone which produces the strength of the moon is white pearl. They should wear white pearl. Wearing of white pearl ensures long life of the wearer and strength of the nerves too. Bad luck will vanish and good luck will be ushered in.

All those born on 3, 12, 21, or 30 of any month are ruled by Jupiter. The gemstone which produces the strength of Jupiter is yellow Pushyaraga. They can wear yellow Pushyaraga. Wearing of yellow Pushyaraga gives strength, beauty, knowledge and fortune to the wearer.

All those born on 4, 13, 22, or 31 of any month are ruled by Uranus. The gemstone which produces the strength of Uranus is Gomeda. They should wear Gomeda. Wearing of Gomeda strengthens the heart. It confers attraction and wealth on the wearer.

All those born on 5, 14, or 23 are ruled by Mercury. The gemstone which produces the strength of Mercury is emerald. They should wear emerald. Wearing of emerald gives self-confidence and good luck to the wearer.

All those born on 6, 15, or 24 of any month are ruled by Venus. The gemstone which produces the strength of Venus is diamond. Wearing of diamond confers wealth and fortune on the wearer.

All those born on 7, 16, or 25 of any month are ruled by Neptune. The gemstone which produces the strength of Uranus is cat's eye. They should wear cat's eye. Wearing of cat's eye gives name, fame, wealth and attraction to the wearer.

All those born on 8, 17, or 26 are ruled by Saturn. The gem which gives the strength of Saturn is blue sapphire.

They should wear blue sapphire. Wearing of blue sapphire will ensure wealth and a long and peaceful life for the wearer.

All those born on 9, 18, or 27 are ruled by Mars. The gem which gives the strength of Mars is red coral. They should wear red coral. Wearing of red coral will give good health, children, success over enemies and good fortune.

Rituals of Wearing Gems

Children below 10 years should not wear gemstones. Patients with prolonged illness should not wear gemstones.

The gemstone should be set in a ring of gold or silver. It is important that all gemstones be kept immersed for at least half an hour in unboiled milk. Afterwards, they should be washed well and worshipped with particular flowers, incense and camphor. The mantras of the planets should be recited 108 times.

For No. 1 People

They should wear ruby on 1st, l0th 19th, or 28th of any month or on Sunday, Tuesday or Thursday. It should be set in a ring of gold mixed with copper. They should keep the gem purified with milk, and offer sandal, red flowers, wheat, incense, and camphor. Then they should recite the Sun mantra 108 times.

Sun Mantra

"OM GRUNI SURYAAYA NAMAHA"

They should wear it in the early morning at the time of sunrise on Sunday, Tuesday or Thursday. The ring should be worn on the ring finger.

For No. 2 People

They should wear pearl or moonstone on 2nd, 11th, 20th, or 29th of any month. It should be set in a ring of silver.

They should keep the gem on a white silk cloth, and offer sandal, white flowers, rice, sugar, incense and camphor. They should recite the Moon mantra 108 times.

Moon Mantra

"OM SOM SOMAAYA NAMAHA"

They should wear it in the early morning of Monday at the time of sunrise. The ring should be worn on the ring finger.

For No. 3 People

They should wear yellow Pushyaraga on 3rd, 12th, 21st, or 30th of any month. It should be set in a ring of gold. They should keep the gem on a yellow silk, and offer sandal, yellow flowers, bengal gram, incense and camphor.

They should recite the mantra of Jupiter 108 times.

Jupiter Mantra

"OM BRUM BRUHASPATHAYE NAMAHA"

They should wear it on the early morning of Thursday, at the time of sunrise. It should be worn on the index finger.

For No. 4 People

They should wear Gomeda on 4th, 13th, 22nd, or 31st of any month. It should be set in a ring of gold or silver.

They should keep the gem on a blue silk, and offer sandal, blue flowers, black gram, incense and camphor. They should recite the Rahu mantra 108 times.

Rahu Mantra

"OM RAAM RAHUVE NAMAHA"

They should wear it on the early morning of Wednesday at the time of sunrise. The ring should be worn on the middle or the little finger.

For No. 5 People

They should wear emerald on the 5th, 14th, or 23rd of any month. It should be set in a ring of gold, silver, or platinum.

They should keep the gem on a green silk, and offer sandal, green leaves, green moong dal, incense and camphor. They should recite the Mercury mantra 108 times.

Mercury Mantra

"OM BHUM BHUDAAYA NAMAHA"

They should wear it on the early morning of Wednesday at the time of sunrise. The ring should be worn on the little finger.

For No. 6 People

They should wear diamond or American diamond on the 6th, 15th, or 24th of any month. It should be set in a ring of silver.

They should keep the gem on a white silk and offer sandal, white flowers, milk, sugar, incense and camphor. They should recite the Venus mantra 108 times.

Venus Mantra

"OM SHUM SHUKRAAYA NAMAHA"

They should wear it on the early morning of Friday at the time of sunrise. The ring should be worn on the middle finger.

For No. 7 People

They should wear cat's eye on the 7th, 16th, or 25th of any month. It should be set in a ring of silver. They should keep the gem on a red silk, offer sandal, red flowers, horse gram, incense and camphor. They should recite the Ketu mantra 108 times.

Ketu Mantra

"OM KEM KETHAVE NAMAHA"

They should wear it on the early morning of Wednesday at the time of sunrise. The ring should be worn on the middle or the little finger.

For No. 8 People

They should wear blue sapphire on 8th, 17th, or 26th of any month. It should be set in a ring of silver. They should keep the gem on a blue silk, offer sandal, blue flowers, incense and camphor. They should recite the Shani mantra 108 times.

Shani Mantra

"OM SHAM SHANAISCHARAAYA NAMAHA"

They should wear it on the early morning of Saturday.

For No. 9 People

They should wear red coral on the 9th, 18th, or 27th of any month. It should be set in a ring of gold mixed with copper. They should keep the gem on a red silk and offer sandal, red flowers, tur dal, incense and camphor. They should recite the Mars mantra 108 times.

Mars Mantra

"OM AM ANGAARAKAAYA NAMAHA"

They should wear it on the early morning of Tuesday at the time of sunrise. The ring should be worn on the ring finger.

9

Remedial Measures to Neutralise Negative Numbers: Mantras, Yantras and Charities

The date of birth is called the ruling number, whereas the gross total of the complete birth dates indicates the number of destiny, which is also called the Fadic number. The Fadic number is the cause of both good and bad events in life.

When we arrange the numerical horoscope, we can understand the strength of planets in our horoscope. If a number is afflicted it is called a negative number. Negative numbers have the power to produce bad effects on the person in whose horoscope they figure.

For an afflicted and negative number, one should perform remedies to the planet represented by that number. If this is done the planet will be pleased and will not produce the bad effects the person dreads and wants to avoid.

Mantras & Charities

Remedies may be sought by reciting the mantras of the hostile planet and giving certain things as alms to that planet as prescribed.

Sun Mantra

Dwi Bhujam, Padma Hastam Cha
Varadam Makutaanvitam
Dyayet Diwaakaram Devam Sarvaabeeshta
Pradaayakam

The following things could be given as alms to the poor: Wheat, jaggery, coconut, coconut oil, almond etc.

Moon Mantra

Jataa Dhaara Shiro Ratnam, Shweta Varnam
Nishaakaram
Dhyayeth Amrutha Sambootham Sarva Kaama Phala
Pradam

The following things could be given as alms to the poor: Milk, rice, silver, milk sweets and water-rich vegetables.

Mars Mantra

Dharani Garbha Sambhotam Vidyuth Kaanthi
Samaprabham
Kumaaram Shakthi Hastham Cha Mangalam
Pranamamyaham

The following things could be given as alms to the poor: Ginger, garlic, pineapple, honey, sindoor etc.

Jupiter Mantra

Hreem, Devaanam Cha Gurum Kanchana
Sannibham
Buddi Bootham Trilokesam Tam Namaami
Bruhaspathim

The following things could be given as alms to the poor: Corn, pomegranate, olive, pepper and vinegar.

Rahu Mantra

Naaga Dwajaaya Vidmahe, Padma Hastaaya Dheemahee,
Tanno Rahu Prachodayat

The following things could be given as alms to the poor: Potato, soap, winter green and charcoal.

Mercury Mantra

Simhaaroodam Chaturbaahum, Kadgacharma Gadaadaram,
Somaputram Mahasowmyam Dyaayet Sarvaardha Siddidam

The following things could be given as alms to the poor: Green cloth or bangles and green leafy vegetables.

Shukra Mantra

Ashwa Dwajjaya Vidmahe, Danur Hastaaya Dheemahi,
Tanno Sukra Prachodayat

The following things could be given as alms to the poor: Curd, ghee, camphor, dhoop and flowers.

Shani Mantra

Neelanjana Samaabaasam Raviputram Yamagrajam,
Chaayaa Maarthaanda Sambootham
Tham Namaami Sanaisharam

The following things could be given as alms to the poor: Black til, black sweets, black cloth and slippers etc.

Ketu Mantra

Om Kem Kethave Namaha

The following things could be given as alms to the poor: Banana, black til, lemon and coffee.

According to *Yantra Chintamani*, the ancient book, yantra for each planet may also be worshipped along with the mantra of that planet for remedial measures. It may also be used as a talisman for wearing on the neck. This will ensure good health, wealth and prosperity.

Yantra of No. 1

6	1	8
7	5	3
2	9	4

Sun Yantra

All those born on 10th, 11th, 19th, or 28th of any month can use this talisman for prosperity. This should be engraved on a gold plate or a ring made of gold. If it is a ring, it should be worn on the ring finger.

Yantra of No. 2

All those born on 2nd, 11th, 20th, or 29th of any month can use this talisman for prosperity.

7	2	9
8	6	4
3	10	5

Moon Yantra

This should be engraved on a silver sheet or a ring made of silver. If it is a ring, it should be worn on the ring finger.

Yantra of No. 3

All those born on 3rd, 12th, 21st or 30th of any month can use this talisman for prosperity.

10	5	12	
11	9	7	Jupiter Yantra
6	13	8	

This should be engraved as a talisman on a gold plate or a ring made of gold. If it is a ring, it should be worn on the first finger.

Yantra of No. 4

All those born on 4th, 13th, 22nd, or 31st of any month can use this Yantra for prosperity.

13	8	15	
14	12	10	Rahu Yantra
9	16	11	

The Yantra should be engraved as a talisman on a tin sheet or a ring made of tin. If it is a ring, wear it on the little finger.

Yantra of No. 5

All those born on 5th, 14th, or 23rd of any month can use this talisman for prosperity.

9	4	11	
10	8	6	Mercury Yantra
5	12	7	

The yantra should be engraved as a talisman on a brass sheet or a ring made of brass. If it is a ring, it should be worn on the little finger.

Yantra of No. 6

All those born on 6th, 15th, or 24th of any month can use this Yantra for prosperity.

11	6	13	
12	10	8	Shukra Yantra
7	14	9	

The Yantra should be engraved as a talisman on a silver sheet or a ring made of silver. If it is a ring, wear it on the middle finger.

Yantra of No. 7

All those born on 7th, 16th, or 25th of any month can wear this talisman for prosperity.

14	9	16	
15	13	11	Ketu Yantra
10	17	12	

This should be engraved as a talisman on a silver sheet or a ring made of silver. If it is a ring, wear it on the middle or the little finger.

Yantra of No. 8

All those born on 8th, 17th, or 26th of any month can wear this talisman for prosperity.

12	7	14	
13	11	9	Shani Yantra
8	15	10	

This should be engraved as a talisman on a zinc sheet or a ring made of zinc. If it is a ring, wear it on the middle finger.

Yantra of No. 9

All those born on 9th, 18th, or 27th of any month can wear this talisman for prosperity.

8	3	10
9	7	5
4	11	6

Mars Yantra

This should be engraved as a talisman on a gold sheet mixed with copper or a ring made of gold and copper. If it is a ring, wear it on the ring finger.

OOO

10

Lucky Business for Various People

The name of the business should be in the lucky numbers. The lucky number is considered according to the date of birth of a person. The lucky number for the establishment should be the proprietor's lucky number or a favourable number. If so, the business will run smoothly. There are so many shops in big cities. So many varieties of clothes manufactured by different mills are sold in each shop. But a crowd is seen only in a few shops. What is the reason? It is because the name-number of that shop has the power to attract people.

Similarly, soaps, detergents, toothpastes, powders etc. are sold under different trademarks. But many people like to purchase only some particular soap or powder with a particular trademark. It does not mean that the soaps and powders with other trademarks are poor in quality. The only reason for this success is the name-number of the trademark. With trademark No. 8, if a man sells a thing related to No. 6, he will face only loss in business. So each number has its own items, and each person should select a business suitable to his own number. The name of the business or trademarks should be in a suitable number.

Each planet is responsible for certain works and certain commodities. We should select our business according to, or compatible with, our own planet, and keep the name of the business and the trademark as per our lucky numbers.

Commodities and Business Suited to Each Person

No. 1

Jewellery, electronic and electrical goods, construction goods, business relating to foreign commodities, advertising, sponsoring of TV programmes, cinema industry, designing and planning, pawn broking and departmental stores.

No. 2

Trades in liquids, milk, ice-cream parlour, pathological laboratory, lab technician, medicine and chemicals, agriculture, timber, coal, mines, acting, art, import and export trade, construction, music, creative art, printing and publishing, caretaker of any organisation, general shop, lawyer, doctor, vegetables, perfumes and consultancy service.

No. 3

Consultancy, advisory service, finance company, chartered accountancy, banking, advertising, music, art, share, chit, coaching centre, cloth business, star hotel, bookshop and running a school.

No. 4

All sorts of machineries, photo studios, hotel, tailoring, photocopy business, electric shop, transport service, automobile, agriculture, real estate, construction, building contract, infotech business, stock exchange broking, leather goods, plastic goods, gas agency, astrology, engineering, designing and TV business.

No. 5

Commercial art, agencies, transport and travel agency, law practice, banking, games and sports organising, STD, courier service, sponsoring TV programmes, advertising, nursery, horticulture, tobacco, aluminium, oil and engineering.

No. 6

Broker's business, estate broker's business, commission agency, all entertainments, fast food, hotel, catering, agriculture, jewellery, piece goods business, dairy farm, fancy bangles, perfumes, toys, dry fruits, bakery, marketing of beauty and luxury items, beauty parlour, creche, paints, music school, library, salts, interior decoration, flowers and poultry farm.

No. 7

Detective service, art and music, fish, film, dairy farm, liquid, rubber, chemicals like soaps, medicines, mining, photo studio, cinema and theatre.

No. 8

Chemicals, iron, brass, bricks, pots, cement, sanitaryware, hardware, timber, coal, photocopy, printing press, DTP, agriculture, transport, travel agency, shoe mart, typewriting institute, oil, screen printing, pesticides, fertiliser, sweater business, shawls, stainless steel and poultry.

No. 9

Printing and publishing, detective service, medicines, sports, electronic goods, metals, food, luxury items, entertainment business, school and educational institutions, plywood, hardware, contract work, chemical items, gas agency, vessel shop etc.

OOO

11

Lucky Numbers for Marriage, Job, Education and Childbirth

Lucky Colours and Days for Marriage

For No. 1 Persons

They should fix the day of marriage on Sunday, Tuesday or Thursday, or on dates 1, 10, or 19. The girl should wear an orange or yellow dress, and sport red flowers in her hair. The bride's mother should serve sweets made of wheat to the bridegroom. Thereby, her planet Sun will be very pleased and will bestow success.

For No. 2 Persons

They should fix the day of marriage on Monday or Friday or on dates 2, 11, 20 or 29 or 6, 15 or 24. The girl should wear cream coloured, light green or light blue dress and use white jasmine flowers for her hair. The bride's mother should serve sweets made of rice to the bridegroom. Thereby, her planet Moon will be pleased and bestow success.

For No. 3 Persons

They should fix the day of marriage on 3rd, 12th, 21st or 30th or on Tuesday, Thursday or Sunday. The girl should wear a yellow dress and use yellow flowers for her hair. The bride's mother should serve plantains or any yellow sweet to the bridegroom. The girl's planet Jupiter will then be pleased to bestow success.

For No. 4 Persons

They should keep the day of marriage on Tuesday or Friday or on dates 6, 15 or 24. The girl should wear a yellow, green or blue dress and use yellow flowers for her hair. The bride's mother should serve brown sweets to the bridegroom or should serve soup in a silver bowl after the sweets. Thereby, her planet Rahu will be pleased to bestow success.

For No. 5 Persons

They should keep the day of marriage on Wednesday or Friday or on dates 5, 14 or 23. The girl should adorn white flowers in her hair and wear a green dress. The bride's people should serve sweets made of milk to the bridegroom. The planet Mercury will then be pleased to bestow success.

For No. 6 Persons

They should keep the day of marriage on Friday or on dates 6, 15 or 24. The girl should wear a blue or rose dress and use white jasmine or rose flowers for her hair. The bride's people should serve gulkand to the bridegroom. Thereby, the planet Venus will be pleased to bestow success.

For No. 7 Persons

They should keep the day of marriage on Monday or Tuesday, or on dates 7, 16 or 25. The girl should wear a yellow dress and use yellow flowers in her hair. The bride's people should serve red or brown sweets to the bridegroom. Thereby, the planet Ketu will be pleased to bestow success and prosperity on them.

For No. 8 Persons

They should keep the day of marriage on Wednesday or Friday, or on dates 5, 6, 14, 15, 23 or 24. The girl should wear a dark-blue dress and use a blue hairpin for her hair. The bride's people should serve sweets made of beetroot. Thereby, her planet Saturn will be pleased to bestow success and prosperity.

For No. 9 Persons

They should keep the day of the marriage on Tuesday or Thursday or on dates 9 or 27. The girl should wear a red dress and sport red flowers or a red pin in her hair. The bride's people should serve red sweets to the bridegroom. Thereby, the planet Mars will be pleased to bestow success and prosperity.

Lucky Numbers for Job and Education

Important applications for job or education should be sent on 10th or 19th of any month, or on Sunday, Tuesday or Thursday, by No. 1 persons.

Likewise, No. 2 persons should apply on dates 2, 11 or 29 or on Monday and No. 3 persons should apply on dates 3, 12, 21 or 30 or on Thursday, Tuesday or Sunday. No. 4 persons should apply on 4th, 13th, 22nd or 31st or on Tuesday or Friday. No. 5 persons should apply on Wednesday or Friday or on dates 5, 14 or 23. No. 6 persons should apply on Tuesday or Friday or on dates 6, 15 or 24. No. 7 persons should apply on Tuesday or Friday or on dates 7, 16 or 25. No. 8 persons should apply on Wednesday or Friday or on dates 5, 6, 14, 15, 23 or 24. No. 9 persons should apply on Tuesday or Thursday or on dates 9 or 27.

If they do so, they will achieve success in their endeavours, whatever the odds.

Lucky Number for Childbirth

Those not blessed with children should keep their lucky names in the Sun's number of Virgo sign. When women come under the fold of the Sun's number 46, they can bear children. The Sun entering Virgo sign of the Zodiac has great significance. This number is believed to have the power to bless a person with children.

OOO

12

Marital Happiness through Numerology

Numerology has its own ways of determining marital compatibility, which does not seem to have been understood by people, owing to their ignorance of this science. From the study of numerology, we can find out whether two individuals, who intend to live together, have natural compatibility. It will also be a good guide, as it will help the two individuals to understand each other thoroughly.

Numerological study helps in psychoanalysis of couples. It is important for both the individuals to understand each other's approach towards life and also each other's likes and dislikes. In the absence of this understanding, it is hard for them to live together happily.

According to the date of birth, everybody should find out towards whom he or she has a natural affinity, and who can be his or her life partner. Even after marriage, some marital problems could and, in fact, do arise on account of incompatibility between the spouses, not obvious to them before marriage.

Remedial Measures through Numerology

If a couple has marital problems on account of incompatibility, we can work on their birth dates and names. If the birth dates match but, even then, the two do not get along well and have quarrels, we can work out the vowels in their names and suggest changes in their names so that, on the mental level, they could have harmony.

Every name has a vibratory number. The vowels and consonants in the names represent the mental and material numbers respectively. The mental number works upon the mind and affects the mind and personality of the individual. Through the consonants we can know the material picture of the individual. Thus the name creates mental vibrations and material vibrations of an individual. These two are governed by the particular planets according to their numbers. If mental vibrations of both individuals are of friendly or favourable planets' numbers, both names emit harmonious vibrations and their radiations are in unison with each other, they sail smoothly in life. If their vibrations are not in unison, the results are bound to be the opposite.

Characters of Individuals Born on Various Numbers

No. 1 Persons

All those born on 1st, 10th, 19th, or 28th of any month come under this class. They are frank, honest and brave. They are egoistic. They have high ideals in life with morals. They come straight to the point and do not beat about the bush. They have self-confidence, courage and originality. They are articulate, but kind and noble-hearted. They are commanding and aristocratic by nature. They love their homes and spend much of their time at home.

No. 2 Persons

All those born on 2nd, 11th, 20th, or 29th of any month come under this class.

They are dreamers! They build castles in the air! They are the emotional, cowardly and homely type. They are sympathetic, affectionate and satisfied with whatever they get from their partners. They will assist their partners. Sometimes they are off mood and edgy and even small matters irritate them and they fight with their partners.

No. 3 Persons

All those born on 3rd, 12th, 21st or 30th of any month come under this class. They are sympathetic and warm. They have high morality. They like peace and harmony. They have self-respect. If they receive any help from others, they feel there is some weakness in them!

They wish to participate in outdoor activities. They have more confidence in themselves.

No. 4 Persons

All those born on 4th, 13th, 22nd, or 31st of any month come under this category.

They are moody, yet reliable and trustworthy. Whenever their mood is upset, it takes them long to return to normal. They are hard workers but suspicious and contradictory by nature. At the same time, they are generous and loving. They are cautious but domineering and fastidious and expect partners to share their ideas. They want all affairs of the home to be run as per their own ideas and cause tension by imposing their will on others.

No. 5 Persons

All those born on 5th, 14th, or 23rd of any month come under this category.

They are active. They expect the same degree of neatness and tidiness from their partners. They are interested in the home as well as the outdoors. They want to see their partners well dressed. They are liberal in spending on clothes and other wants of the family. They easily forget their difficulties. They always like changes in environment, ideas, dress and in running their homes.

No. 6 Persons

All those born on 6th, 15th, or 24th of any month come under this category.

They are passionate, fond of new clothes and like to put on costly dresses. They like to wear ornaments. They expect their partners to be neat, charming and graceful. They love their partners, home and children. They are kind, generous, devoted and sympathetic. They never save money. They spend their earnings on whatever interests them. They have a sharp memory and an unduly bloated ego.

No. 7 Persons

All those born on 7th, 16th, or 25th of any month come under this category.

They are stubborn and disagree with the opinions of others. They don't mix with people. They want freedom and do not hesitate even to change traditions when necessary. They seem mysterious to others. They are suspicious and critical. This creates tension in the family.

No. 8 Persons

They have an extreme sense of discipline and duty. They are contradictory persons with a series of different opinions. They are mostly solitary and melancholy. They display caution and care in taking decisions. They are orthodox, and never adopt modern ideas in dress at home or in public places. They have controlling power.

No. 9 Persons

They are brave and courageous. They easily adapt and gear up to any circumstances. They have endurance. They will more likely exercise severity than kindness. They are always aggressive and will not stop until they achieve their goal. They don't accept defeat. They seem to be born fighters. Despite a foul temper, they lead a good married life and love children and the family.

According to the birth dates, the compatible and incompatible matches for each person are given below:

Birth No. of Person	Compatible Nos.	Incompatible Nos.	Neutral Nos.
1	2, 3, 6, 7, 9	4, 5	8
2	1, 2, 4, 6, 9	3, 5, 8	7
3	1, 6, 7, 9	2, 8	1, 4, 5
4	2, 4, 6, 7	1, 8	5, 9, 3
5	6	2, 5, 7, 8, 1	9, 3, 4
6	1, 2, 3, 4, 5, 6, 9	—	7, 8
7	1, 3, 4, 7, 9	5	8, 2, 6
8	—	2, 3, 4, 5, 8, 9	7, 1
9	1, 2, 3, 6, 7, 9	8	4, 5

Remedial Measures for Marital Harmony through Gems

Apart from adjusting the mental vibrational numbers of their names, there are also remedial measures through the use of gems. Couples who suffer from incompatible alliances should wear suitable gems. By wearing gems the bad effects of those planets are then minimised, and good and favourable effects may be produced.

The selection of gems should be done carefully. In numerology, the planetary position of a person should first be examined. Next, the house of marriage and married life should be carefully studied. Then, according to the strengths, afflictions and negativity of the planets, gems should be selected. These are done through numerological horoscopes.

If the Sun produces evil effects on marital happiness, peridot should be worn. But before that, we have to consider the position of the Sun and Venus in the horoscope to get the correct picture. This is very important. In the same way, 'turquoise' may be given to the person to whom Venus causes disappointments in marital happiness. It can work like magic! Moonstone and green onyx also play important roles in producing marital happiness.

Therefore, the selection of the perfect gem for conjugal happiness should be done by a numerologist.

Remedial Measures to Marital Happiness through Mantra

There are also some remedies through mantras. If there are fights, clashes and misunderstandings, or if circumstances cause a break-up in the relationship, apart from wearing specific gems and altering their names, the couple may also pray to Lakshmi-Ganapathi and recite the Lakshmi-Ganapathi Mantra. This is a powerful mantra and can produce harmonious relations among the couple. The husband or wife can recite this mantra and pray to God. Many persons have benefitted by doing so.

Method of Praying

Keep a Lakshmi-Ganapathi picture or Yantra. If there is no picture or Yantra, worship the same through a lamp. Light the lamp with five faces, and pray to the lamp assuming it to be Lakshmi-Ganapathi. Keep a piece of grass or Tulsi on the lamp and recite the mantra 108 times daily.

Lakshmi-Ganapathi Mantra

OM SREEM HREEM KLEEM KLOWN
NAMO BHAGAVATHYAI VIBHOOTHYAI,
OM SREEM HREEM KLEEM
KLOWN GAM GANAPATHAYE NAMAHA

OOO

13

Meanings of Alphabets

A denotes: Creativity, initiative, will power, ambition, successful domination, constructive attitude, positive mind and egoism.

B denotes: Shy, timid, imaginative, cooperative, moody, emotional and introspective.

C denotes: Healthy, optimistic, positive, beautiful, energetic, successful, intellectual, wise, anxious, tense and afraid.

D denotes: Self-sufficient, thoughtful, materialistic, tolerant, steady and slow but hardworking.

E denotes: Balanced, energetic, learned, talented in writing, intellectual, eloquent, creative, artistic, enthusiastic, famous.

F denotes: Loving, affectionate, devoted to family, patient, responsible, protective, quiet, simple and harmonious.

G denotes: Introspective, analytical, clever, observant, attentive, intuitive, impulsive, flexible, reasoning and uncontrollable.

H denotes: Impressive, firm, balanced, calm, self-sufficient and materialistic.

I denotes: Altruistic, sympathetic, affectionate, loving, sensitive, impatient, intense, alert, self-reliant, egoistic, rebellious and learned.

J denotes: Articulate, friendly, novel, new in ideas, bright in outlook, artistic, prosperous, magnetic, good looking and original.

K denotes: Magnetic personality, patient, helpful, enthusiastic and culture-oriented.

L denotes: Materialistic, aspiring, reasoning, analytical, logical, convincing, active, versatile, successful, public, insightful and understanding.

M denotes: Noble, undefeatable, moody, strong of character and strong in mind.

N denotes: Intellectual, slow, wasting talent, emotional and lucky.

O denotes: Introspective, disciplined, depressed, affectionate, home-loving, exaggerated, secretive and conservative.

P denotes: Strong, perceptive, clear-sighted, egoistic, successful, concentrated, separate, strong willed, balanced.

Q denotes: Firm, successful, powerful, strong, strong willed, hopeful and good in organising.

R denotes: Great strength, impulsive and unsympathetic.

S denotes: Friendly, sensitive, accommodative, inconsistent and confused.

T denotes: Sacrificing, spiritual, anxious, highly ambitious, kind to others, frustrated, selfless, cooperative, feminine, devoted, munificent and generous.

U denotes: Imaginative, romantic, gifted and fearing.

V denotes: Receptive, grasping, wise, well placed, commanding, hardworking and skilled or masterly in planning.

W denotes: Changing, unorthodox, dynamic, fast, vain, interested in travel, exciting, adventurous, eager, enthusiastic, risky, tasteful and ambitious.

X denotes: Depressed, exaggerated about difficulties, delayed, responsible, attractive and spiritual.

Y denotes: Mystic, secretive, emotional, independent, separate or divisive.

Z denotes: Resolute in character, fixed, helpful, respected, great and potent.

OOO

14

Repetition of Alphabets

If an alphabet occurs several times in a name, it is indicative of a particular character.

If Letters A, I, J, Y and Q Occur Repeatedly in a Name

It makes the person courageous, original, domineering and strong headed. It could mean the chance for recognition, struggling for independence and freedom, higher status, cooperative nature, progress in business and craze about money and power.

If B, R and K Occur Repeatedly in a Name

It makes the person very sensitive and with an inferiority complex. He is likely to be cowardly, emotional, musical and artistic. Besides, the person is helpful to others, tactful, cooperative and patient.

If C, G, S and L Occur Repeatedly in a Name

It makes the person very imaginative, artistic and talented. It gives talent for self-expression through words or writings or in art, music and business. It also makes the person selfish, lacking concentration, wasteful of energy through pursuit of pleasures and indiscipline.

If D, M and T Occur Repeatedly in a Name

It makes the person work hard, expand business, manage finances or property matters, take responsibilities towards relatives. It necessarily slows up progress.

If E, N, H and X Occur Repeatedly in a Name

It makes the person successful in legal and public works or in sales promotion. If the above alphabets are repeated seven times or more in the name, it is above average. It denotes high living with drinks, food and sex. This can lead to problems, and make the person irresponsible in family life. Sudden and unexpected happenings could lead to chaos and turmoil.

If V, U and W Occur Repeatedly in a Name

It encourages artistic talents, humanitarianism, sense of responsibility, helpful nature, love of domestic life, social recognition and popularity. There are outings, travels and social activities.

If O and Z Occur Repeatedly in a Name

It makes the person ponder, research, study, meditate, search for truth and remain aloof, away from the crowd and away from problems of relatives etc.

If F and P Occur Repeatedly in a Name

It sharpens business acumen and strengthens power and position. Other things on the cards are:

Lack of domestic happiness, travel for business, heavy expenses and dealings in property.

15

Business Partnership

Matching of numbers in business is different from marriage matching. In marriage problems, the inner consciousness of the number is related to the persons. But in business, the outer consciousness of the number is related to the persons.

If two persons are to be partners in business, we should be assured about the suitability of their numbers.

For No. 1 Persons

No. 1 and No. 1 Combination

This simply won't work. Both have leadership qualities and aspirations. Each will expect the other to follow him. They pull in different ways. Hence the combination is doomed to fail.

No. 1 and No. 2 Combination

This combination would appear to be good. No. 2 can cooperate with No. 1 faithfully. No. 1 is authoritative and impatient while No. 2 cooperates well and acts patiently. So the combination can work and achieve success.

No 1. and No. 3 Combination

This is a successful combination. No. 3 is brilliant and goes about the works of No. 1 with artistic talent and with a nimble mind, which are favourable for business dealings and marketing.

No. 1 and No. 4 Combination

This combination cannot be successful because No. 1 is agile, quick-witted and has new ideas. But No. 4 is slow and lethargic with very limited ideas.

No. 1 and No. 5 Combination

Both are quick in action and adventurous, and they can make a successful combination. But No. 5 is rather fickle and is anything but steadfast. This is his only failing whereas No. 1 has a steady mind.

No. 1 and No. 6 Combination

This is a successful combination. No. 6 has more enthusiasm besides talent. No. 1 is a great planner. Hence this will be a performing team!

No. 1 and No. 7 Combination

No. 1 is authoritative, works assiduously and acts with earnestness. But No. 7 is philosophical, lonely and may not take keen interest in the financial growth of the firm.

No. 1 and No. 8 Combination

This is a good combination. Both have ambitions and steadfast minds. Both are intelligent, persevering and can surmount any obstacle. So the combination is successful for expansion of business.

No. 1 and No. 9 Combination

This is a good combination too. Both are ambitious and hardworking. Both have steady minds, originality and leadership. The talent of No. 9 can bring goodwill to the business.

For No. 2 Persons

No. 2 and No. 1 Combination

(See No. 1 and No. 2 combination).

No. 2 and No. 2 Combination

A very good combination. Both are likeminded with common interests and mutual understanding. So, the partnership will work smoothly.

No. 2 and No. 3 Combination

This is a successful combination. No. 3 is ambitious, brilliant and knows his mind. But No. 2 has no such knowledge. No. 3 provides security to No. 2 and thus commands the respect of others and feels comfortable and at ease.

No. 2 and No. 4 Combination

This is a successful combination too. No. 4 provides security to No. 2 and No. 2 completes an assignment as a faithful follower.

No. 2 and No. 5 Combination

This is not a good combination. No. 5 is fast and quick, while No. 2 is too slow. No. 5 has adaptability while No. 2 is not so.

No. 2 and No. 6 Combination

A good combination! The cooperative spirit of No. 2 and sense of responsibility of No. 6 will work wonderfully well. This will be a performing combination indeed!

No. 2 and No. 7 Combination

This is a good combination. No. 2 is quiet, diplomatic and imaginative, while No. 7 is secretive, aloof, and good in specialisation. Hence the combination can be successful, each complementing the other.

No. 2 and No. 8 Combination

No. 8 is a hard worker, ambitious, strong headed and commanding. No. 8 can direct the business and No. 2 will follow peacefully. So this combination is bound to do well.

No. 2 and No. 9 Combination

It is a successful combination, because of the high talents of No. 9 and excellent cooperation of No. 2.

For No. 3 Persons

No. 3 and No. 1 Combination

No. 3 and No. 2 Combination

(See the No. 2 and No. 1, No. 2 and No. 3 combinations.)

No. 3 and No. 3 Combination

Both have the same characteristics. They have high sensitivity, which can spoil the situation. Thereby they may lose business opportunities. Thus, it is anything but a successful combination.

No. 3 and No. 4 Combination

No. 3 is very intelligent and daring. He is game for taking risks. But No. 4 cannot take any risk. This can create differences of opinion. Hence, there is nothing much to commend about this team!

No. 3 and No. 5 Combination

This is a mixed combination. It is neither a successful nor an unsuccessful combination. The hasty and excited nature of No. 5 and the sensitive and dominating nature of No. 3 could cause certain problems and friction.

No. 3 and No. 6 Combination

This is a good combination. The soft-spoken No. 3 and selfless No. 6 could prove a performing team!

No. 3 and No. 7 Combination

This is a good combination too. The pleasant nature of 3 and the intelligence of No. 7 could prove a successful combination.

No. 3 and No. 8 Combination

This is a strong and successful combination. No. 8 is an executive with efficiency and No. 3 with his pleasant way of speaking is sure to prove an asset in marketing and sales promotion!

No. 3 and No. 9 Combination

This does not appear to be a performing combination for promoting business. No. 3 has a charming and pleasant way of talking but is not likely to take business seriously. No. 9 is a thinker but performs rather dismally. How can such a combination be expected to deliver the goods?

For No. 4 Persons

No. 4 and No. 1 Combination

(See No. 1 and No. 4 combination).

No. 4 and No. 2 Combination

(See No. 2 and No. 4 combination).

No. 4 and No. 3 Combination

(See No. 3 and No. 4 combination).

No. 4 and No. 4 Combination

This is a very successful combination! Both are materialistic, cautious about finances, and able administrators. The business is bound to flourish!

No. 4 and No. 5 Combination

This does not look like a good combination. No. 5 can make good business and take risks restlessly. But No. 4 cannot gear up to the challenges. He will very likely feel ill at ease with the dynamic No. 5. The team may simply not take off!

No. 4 and No. 6 Combination

This appears a promising combination! Both of them are loyal, careful in money matters, and responsible people. The business will certainly look up!

No. 4 and No. 7 Combination

This appears a very promising combination for success. No. 4 can do financial and administrative work very well indeed, while No. 7, an intellectual, has ideas. This can improve business remarkably well.

No. 4 and No. 8 Combination

This is a successful combination. No. 4 is a strenuous worker who will nurture the business well. No. 8 is a good planner, director and organiser with a materialistic mind. Together, they will prove a powerful team!

No. 4 and No. 9 Combination

Nothing much can be expected of this team. No. 4 has a steady mind, feels confident and secure and is materialistic. But No. 9 likes only charitable and philanthropic activities. Their interests are very different. So this combination is bound to fail on account of different pulls. Their worst weakness is woeful lack of cohesion and commonality of ideas.

For No. 5 Persons

No. 5 and No. 1 Combination

(See No. 1 and No. 5 combination).

No. 5 and No. 2 Combination

(See No. 2 and No. 5 combination).

No. 5 and No. 3 Combination

(See No. 3 and No. 5 combination).

No. 5 and No. 4 Combination

(See No. 4 and No. 5 combination).

No. 5 and No. 5 Combination

This is one of the worst combinations that can be thought of. Both are restless, excited and hasty and both cherish freedom. They are certain to find each other a threat and consider each other disagreeable. They cannot get along at all and so will mess up the business.

No. 5 and No. 6 Combination

We can expect great things from this team! No. 6 is a self-propelled, broad-minded and balanced person. No. 5 is clever and talented. The business is bound to look up with mutual understanding between them.

No. 5 and No. 7 Combination

This is not a good combination. No. 5 is easily excited and dynamic. He is sure to fret about his rather slow and non-performing partner. Their coming together is unlikely to help business!

No. 5 and No. 8 Combination

These don't appear to be a performing team at all. No. 5 is original, freedom loving and adaptable, while No. 8 is ambitious, steady and aggressive. The two cannot be a successful combination at all.

No. 5 and No. 9 Combination

No. 5's resourcefulness and flair for public relations are sure to give No. 9 a good position. At the same time No. 9's intuition and knowledge are sure to help No. 5 too. They may prove complementary to each other. Together, they can do very well indeed!

For No. 6 Persons

No. 6 and No. 1 Combinaton

(See No. 1 and No. 6 combination).

No. 6 and No. 2 Combination

(See No. 2 and No. 6 combination).

No. 6 and No. 3 Combination

(See No. 3 and No. 6 combination).

No. 6 and No. 4 Combination

(See No. 4 and No. 6 combination).

No. 6 and No. 5 Combination

(See No. 5 and No. 6 combination).

No. 6 and No. 6 Combination

This promises to be an extremely successful combination. Both are balanced and self-propelled and they can be expected to fare very well in any venture.

No. 6 and No. 7 Combination

This is the worst combination that can be thought of. No. 6 is active and creative, while No. 7 is reserved and aloof. They have nothing at all in common and may feel ill at ease with each other. The business, in such circumstances, may prove a dismal failure.

No. 6 and No. 8 Combination

This is a very successful combination. No. 8 is a good planner, director and administrator, while No. 6 is efficient in managing the firm and in dealing with people and he, furthermore, can be expected to be creative. So they may support each other very well indeed!

No. 6 and No. 9 Combination

This would appear to be a moderately successful combination. No. 6 is peaceful, balanced and highly creative by nature, while No. 9 is intelligent and nimble minded. Hence the team can be expected to deliver the goods, minor drawbacks, if any, notwithstanding.

For No. 7 Persons

No. 7 and No. 1 Combination

(See No. 1 and No. 7 combination).

No. 7 and No. 2 Combination

(See No. 2 and No. 7 combination).

No. 7 and No. 3 Combination

(See No. 3 and No. 7 combination).

No. 7 and No. 4 Combination

(See No. 4 and No. 7 combination).

No. 7 and No. 5 Combination

(See No. 5 and No. 7 combination).

No. 7 and No. 6 Combination

(See No. 6 and No. 7 combination).

No. 7 and No. 7 Combination

This does not appear to be a successful combination for business. Neither of them is materialistic or practical. Hence they are bound to fail in business.

No. 7 and No. 8 Combination

This is a moderately successful combination. The guidance of No. 7 and the hard work of No. 8 can be expected to complement each other and help business somewhat.

No. 7 and No. 9 Combination

There is no way this combination can work! Both No. 7 and No. 9 are philanthropic. No. 7 is aloof and imaginative, while No. 9 can think about the welfare of others rather than about the success of the business. How can a team like this promote business?

For No. 8 Persons

No. 8 and No. 1 Combination

(See No. 1 and No. 8 combination).

No. 8 and No. 2 Combination

(See No. 2 and No. 8 combination).

No. 8 and No. 3 Combination

(See No. 3 and No. 8 combination).

No. 8 and No. 4 Combination

(See No. 4 and No. 8 combination).

No. 8 and No. 5 Combination

(See No. 5 and No. 8 combination).

No. 8 and No. 6 Combination

(See No. 6 and No. 8 combination).

No. 8 and No. 7 Combination

(See No. 7 and No. 8 combination).

No. 8 and No. 8 Combination

This can lead to a resounding success or to an utter failure because both are selfish, and will do anything for achieving their selfish goals. They often don't heed each other's advice and are even rude to each other. If they cooperate with each other and judge people and events sensibly, the business could look up. But two selfish and self-centred people are unlikely to act discreetly. The business is bound to suffer.

No. 8 and No. 9 Combination

This is not a successful combination either. The materialistic mind of No. 8 and the spiritual mind of No. 9 will never cooperate and this is sure to give rise to conflicts between them.

For No. 9 Persons

No. 9 and No. 1 Combination

(See No. 1 and No. 9 combination).

No. 9 and No. 2 Combination

(See No. 2 and No. 9 combination).

No. 9 and No. 3 Combination

(See No. 3 and No. 9 combination).

No. 9 and No. 4 Combination

(See No. 4 and No. 9 combination).

No. 9 and No. 5 Combination

(See No. 5 and No. 9 combination).

No. 9 and No. 6 Combination

(See No. 6 and No. 9 combination).

No. 9 and No. 7 Combination

(See No. 7 and No. 9 combination).

No. 9 and No. 8 Combination

(See No. 8 and No. 9 combination).

No. 9 and No. 9 Combination

This combination could prove successful if the company is philanthropic or in humanitarian service. But if it is a commercial business, this combination cannot be successful.

16

Meaning of Compound Numbers

All the numbers from 10 upwards become compound numbers and have a meaning of their own. The practical meanings of the compound numbers from 10 to 100 are furnished here.

No. 10

This number is very successful. It exudes self-confidence. Business will be successful especially in the matter of trademarks. This number evokes enthusiasm.

No. 11

This number ensures success for those who wish to join the film industry. Success will be assured for budding actors and actresses. But success will be shortlived. Gradually, the good fortune will wear off.

No. 12

A very bad number. This number indicates accident, disease, cunning and secret enemies. People with this number cannot have peace of mind.

No. 13

This number is very unfortunate too. This has been proved time and again. This is a forbidden number. In business, although it gives success in the beginning, slowly it can drag the person into litigation or create many difficult problems, which cannot be solved and in the end make the person close down the business. He will increasingly face financial loss, ill health and other problems. He remains a very embittered man.

No. 14

This number is successful, particularly for the cinema field, art and literature. But this number can give natural troubles like asthma and other debilitating diseases. So it is a good number for business only but a bad one in other ways.

No. 15

This is the most successful number. Success in business, domestic life and finance is indicated. It is good as a trademark number. Early marriage is also on the cards.

No. 16

This number is successful for business. But it can cause ill health, disease, prolonged illness, accidents etc. If a problem is created, it will stay put throughout life. It will leave a deep scar on the victim. It almost wrecks a person.

No. 17

This is a successful number for business. But it cannot be suited to all. If suited, it gives financial success and will power. Otherwise, it causes poverty and deprivation!

No. 18

This is an unfortunate number. It denotes disease and accident. This number creates bad effects on the human mind. Wherever they go, they will experience misunderstandings and clashes. Nobody treats them in a friendly way. They are subjugated instead!

No. 19

This number has an attraction. It can give wealth, harmony, name, fame, position and authority. It is a very successful number, and has an intense vibrational power.

No. 20

This number is lucky for business, especially ones like liquor, chemicals, provision shop, super bazaar and so forth. It induces a calm nature. Sometimes, health may be affected. Particularly, mental strain may be caused.

No. 21

This number can make one a writer and even a great scholar. Wealth and prosperity are also indicated. But, sometimes, it can cause obstacles and trials in the early part. Yet, it is a successful number for all businesses.

No. 22

This is a very successful number, when Rahu becomes the bestower of fortunes. This number can give plenty of wealth, force one into illegal ways of earning and duplicity. Litigations are also on the cards for this number. But this number is successful for limited companies in the field of heavy machineries and heavy vehicles. This can come up well within a short period. But, in course of time, this number can produce internal problems or problems with the government and so on.

No. 23

A successful number indicating wealth, honour, and prosperity. This is a very successful number for business and trademarks.

No. 24

A successful number. This number can confer all kinds of happiness, wealth, etc. at an average level. Success in problems with the government is also indicated.

No. 25

This is a very successful number. This can confer wealth and prosperity. It can create a spiritual mind as well.

No. 26

If it is suited, this number can ensure success at the topmost level. But it is very rare. Generally, this is known to cause failures, sorrows, diseases, debts, disappointments and a narrow mind. Whatever work they undertake, they may encounter obstacles that make the chances of success rather bleak.

No. 27

Quick temper and rashness are seen. This may ensure wealth and honour. This number can give fortitude, strength and energy. Spiritual outlook may be fostered too!

No. 28

This gives success in the beginning but the end is a failure. This number is under the influence of Saturn.

No. 29

This is good for business, particularly in grains and pulses. The number may produce a restless mind. Sometimes, in extreme cases, it may even lead to neurotic disorders. In domestic life, this can create confusion.

No. 30

It is a successful number but a very slow and calm one. This can give knowledge, courage and spiritual outlook. Moderate prosperity can be expected.

No. 31

This number has extraordinary powers. If this number is suitable, it can take a person to the very pinnacle. Otherwise, it can push him into loss of position, difficulties in the profession, loss of prestige and so on.

No. 32

This is a very successful number. Under the influence of this number, even a common man can achieve success. This is the seat of learning. So, education will flourish well under this number. This number has the power of attraction.

No. 33

This number is a successful one. One can achieve wealth, health and education through this number. This is considered a Lakshmi number in the Shastras.

No. 34

This number cannot give any material benefit. The person may even lose masculinity or manhood. He may become quarrelsome.

No. 35

This number drags men into litigation and controversies. This may create confusion. In services, this can cause or occasion suspension, dismissal from service and so forth.

No. 36

This is a successful number for business. But, in domestic life, this number may create confusion, quarrels and a deeply disturbed family life.

No. 37

This is a very successful number. It is a very hot number too. The number may create an unfavourable situation at office and may even trigger suspension or dismissal of the person from service, or due to hard feelings they themselves may resign from the service. The health of a life partner may also be affected.

No. 38

This number can yield success in the beginning but, eventually, will occasion defeat with loss of respect and wealth too.

No. 39

This is a very successful number for film directors, team work etc. This gives extraordinary knowledge. But progress may be slow!

No. 40

It is not a very fortunate number from a materialistic point of view. It represents loneliness and isolation from people. Troubles through litigation, accusation, blame and dishonour are indicated. But this number is most successful for business. Heavy machineries, automobiles, transport business etc. will run successfully under the influence of this number.

No. 41

This is a very successful and welcome number. It has the power to confer royal honour, position and wealth. This number is most successful for trademarks etc. This can give quick success in all ventures.

No. 42

This number represents a very happy life and wealth. Honourable friends, position and success in public life are also indicated. It confers sound health as well.

No. 43

This is an unfortunate number. It represents revolution, confusion, failure, loss of position and what not.

No. 44

This number indicates deception, trials, tribulations, unexpected dangers, unreliable friends, grief and betrayal in married life and other relationships.

No. 45

This is a successful number. It indicates the promise of authority, power and command. Wealth and honour are indicated. Mental worry and restlessness are also occasioned. This number also has curative powers.

No. 46

This is a fortunate number. Success in friendship, love and partnership are all indicated. Those who are not blessed with children get children. This number confers all prosperities.

No. 47

This is not a fortunate number. Deception, sudden dangers, trials, and grief through a life partner are on the cards.

No. 48

This number is neither fortunate nor unfortunate. This is not a worldly number and it represents faith in religion.

No. 49

This is a mental number and indicates restlessness. Saturn plays a dominant role in their lives. Else, why are they so restless?

No. 50

This is a successful number. Knowledge of mathematics, physical science and astrology is indicated. Instances of success in literary field and earnings through intellectual pursuits are seen.

No. 51

This is a very successful number. This can take the person to the topmost position. At the same time, it indicates troubles through secret enemies.

No. 52

A very successful number for business but a rather slow one. Loss of position after 40 years is indicated. This may give spiritual outlook and knowledge. But this number cannot be utilised fully.

No. 53

This is an unfortunate number. It indicates obstacles, sudden deception etc. But it can bring name and fame to those who are in public life.

No. 54

This is a successful and strong number. But the end will be violent. No family happiness is indicated. This can cause extreme cunning. Troubles through relatives could also be expected.

No. 55

This is a very successful number. This can give knowledge, intelligence, name and fame. But it is a very risky number. This number has the power to endanger one's life, if not suited to a person.

No. 56

It is a successful number. Business may flourish under this number, particularly grains, pulses and other provisional items.

It is good for writers and poets but, generally, not so good for others. This is suitable for a nickname. This can make the mind restless.

No. 57

This is an unfortunate number. Hardships and troubles are on the cards. This number cannot give so much trouble to those who lead a spiritual existence without expecting anything from life.

No. 58

This is a powerful number. But this can give dangerous results and even cause monetary loss, danger, scandal, enmity and other problems.

No. 59

This is a successful number. Earning through intellectual pursuits is also indicated. Success through writings, publishing books etc. is also seen. Good profits may accrue. More cunning is seen. Stomach, liver and spleen complaints are indicated.

No. 60

This is an average number. Generally, it is neither successful nor unsuccessful. This can ensure family happiness, success in an artistic field etc.

No. 61

There is no family happiness and domestic peace under this number for people in business. This is a modestly successful number.

No. 62

This is an unfortunate number but is good for politicians. Lies come naturally to them and they can be expected to be tactful, however hopeless the situation.

No. 63

This is a very confusing number. This can do both good and bad. This can affect the health of the person and bring about loss in business. It may even wipe out domestic happiness altogether. Bad habits may be formed. Aimless wandering is also on the cards.

No. 64

This is a successful number. They may be successful in the beginning. But later on, one may encounter disappointment, blame, back-stabbing and just about anything.

No. 65

This is a somewhat successful number. In the beginning, it works actively enough. But, gradually, it becomes dull and slow. Many ups and downs could arise. Financial trouble may have to be faced!

No. 66

This is a very successful number. It can ensure success to suitable persons and unsuitable persons alike. If suitable persons keep this number, it can ensure success in the matter of wealth and prosperity. But that success will be shortlived. Within a short while, negative results show up. So they can keep this number for their initial success and within some months, they should change it to their suitable number. If they do so, they can flourish very well, without any break, and success will come to them consistently.

No. 67

This is neither a successful nor unsuccessful number. This can impact a person in a spiritual way. It can give physical and mental hurt, and dissuade a person from attachments and love in domestic life. Then, it will indeed be an immense gain on a spiritual plane!

No. 68

This is a very bad number. This can ruin domestic happiness, create worries, financial problems, business troubles etc. This is under the control of Saturn. It can spur a person on the spiritual path.

No. 69

This is a modestly successful number. This can ensure success in art, writing etc. This gives enjoyment in life. But regular medical check-ups are required.

No. 70

This is a barren number. There is no happiness and prosperity. Life will be miserable. Nothing good can be expected at all.

No. 71

This is not a fortunate number on the material side. This may impart a philosophical outlook. But it may ensure success in business.

No. 72

This is a very successful number: Wealth, honour and courage are indicated. The blessings of God are on this number. It is a truly successful number for business.

No. 73

This is an intelligent number. Success in business is indicated. A business of electronic or electrical goods can be very successful under this number. Business relating to machineries will also come up well under this number. This number can produce a strong mind and attractive personality, ensure popularity and confer wealth.

No. 74

This number creates confusion in the mind. The mind will be wavering and disturbed. But this can ensure talent for good speech and the arts and refine literary tastes as well.

No. 75

This number ensures taste in art and literature. This gives the blessings of Goddess Saraswathi. This may make a person frank and outspoken.

No. 76

This number can give success in the beginning in an adventurous way. But, in the middle, sudden loss and litigation could take place. If it is a business, it may close down mid-way.

No. 77

This is a spiritual number. This can ensure spiritual knowledge and take the person on the spiritual path. It is a very difficult number for human beings.

No. 78

This number is a very refined number and may make one rich. But it is a spiritual and wisdom conferring number, and not very suitable for worldly life.

No. 79

This is a successful number. This can win over enemies, and the success will be permanent. This number has the power to charm people.

No. 80

This is the number of magical studies. If a person wants to study the science of magic and practise it, this number is ideal. This can lead one along the philosophical and religious path.

No. 81

This is a good number. One can reach the highest position. Political success is indicated. One can achieve the topmost position in politics. One can rise in life easily under the influence of this number.

No. 82

This number is successful. It confers knowledge, ability and intelligence. Good position and an established status in the financial field are indicated.

No. 83

This is a good number. This can give authority, wealth, prestige and honour. Financial ascendancy will be permanent and enduring!

No. 84

This number is not merely good materially but can ensure spiritual advancement as well.

No. 85

This is a successful number. But it only acts slowly. It can drive away evil spirits. High position in medical, technical and police lines is also on the cards.

No. 86

This number is rather slow in conferring benefits. One can achieve success slowly but steadily. Defeated persons may gain victory gradually.

No. 87

This is not a worldly number. It is a spiritual one. Surrender to God will see one through trials.

No. 88

This is a moderately successful number. Success in agriculture and business is indicated.

No. 89

This number is good. It can ensure success in all matters. Wealth and riches are indicated. But some accidents may occur in the beginning.

No. 90

This is a full number and a spiritual one. They should try hard to achieve success.

No. 91

This is a good number. Success in property matters, particularly lands and buildings, is indicated. It makes one go on visits to holy places and fosters devotion towards God.

No. 92

This is an average number. They can win over enemies and achieve good health and wealth.

No. 93

Success in the literary fields and writings is indicated. They like freedom. They are intelligent. But married life will not ensure any happiness.

No. 94

This can ensure success in business.

No. 95

This gives a commanding nature and sizeable wealth.

No. 96

It makes a person engage in public service and humanitarian activities.

No. 97

This is a successful number. Acquisition of properties and spiritual progress are indicated. This gives success in profession and a stable financial position.

No. 98

This imparts knowledge and intelligence. But they should compulsorily pray. This can ensure a philosophical outlook.

No. 99

This is not a worldly number. If they pray with all their heart, they can achieve success.

No. 100

This imparts knowledge. Wealth and ability are also on the cards.

OOO

Conclusion

Numerology and Your Luck

In this book I have described the method of choosing a lucky name for each person according to the Zodiac sign. No doubt this can bring fortunes; but the most efficient way of fixing one's lucky name is according to the numerical horoscope. By means of the numerical horoscope, we can know the running period, the planetary position of each number, and which number will fetch the best fortune for fixing one's name and so forth. In this way, I have fixed names for thousands of my clients and each and every person attained success.

A particular name was fixed for a client to confer a male issue by omission of a single letter 'E'. Within a year, the client's desire was fulfilled. A client whose divorce case was pending in the court for over nine years had his case settled within three months after adding the letter 'A'. A separated couple came together again. A penniless man became the owner of a big transport company. Several delayed marriages were settled. All these happened through fixing fortunate names by the above method. All these instances reveal the power of numbers or numerology. I fervently hope this book will decisively reverse persistent ill luck and ensure success for everyone!

V RAJSUSHILA
(Numerologist)

Books on Astrology, Numerology & Palmistry
LAL KITAB A Rare Book On Astrology
240/-
(Hardbound)
Astrology for Layman
80/-
Explore the Power of Astrology
96/-
Salient features of Indian Astrology
96/-
Explore the Power of Astrology Trikona
125/-
Marriage-Matching Astrologically
80/-
Horoscope Reading Made Easy and Self-Learning
150/-
Healing Power of HYPNOTISM
150/-
Numerology of Romance Love by Numbers
80/-
NUMEROLOGY
96/-
Palmistry for Beginners
88/-
Hypnotism for Beginners
75/-
PRACTICAL HYPNOTISM
75/-
PRACTICAL PALMISTRY
80/-
INSTANT HAND WRITING ANALYSIS
96/-
Postage: Rs. 15/- each book. Every subsequent book: Rs. 5/- extra